Bugs, Bull, & Rats

An Insider's account of how the Mob Self-destructed

Frank Palmeri

Brighton Publishing LLC
435 N. Harris Drive
Mesa, AZ 85203

Bugs, Bull, & Rats

An Insider's account of how the Mob Self-destructed

Frank Palmeri

Brighton Publishing LLC
435 N. Harris Drive
Mesa, AZ 85203
www.BrightonPublishing.com

ISBN 13: 978-1-62183-282-9

ISBN 10: 1-62183-282-1

Copyright © 2015

Printed in the United States of America

First Edition

Cover Design: Tom Rodriguez

Preface

Frank Palmeri has a story to tell. After serving a long prison stretch, he returned to a city where the Mafia was now a shadow of the dominant force it once was. So many mobsters had been imprisoned. So many more were cooperating with the government to send even more to prison.

His world as a made member of the Mafia had changed. Since New York's Five Families were organized in the cloak of secrecy in 1931, the world had changed. The secrets of this once secret society are now mass-media fodder in books, movies, TV and the Internet. After eighty years, change has challenged *omertà*, the Mafia code of silence and loyalty. There is little silence anymore.

Omertà was held sacred by all those who swore to the oath. It was never revealed until October 1963, when a former Genovese Family solider, Joseph Valachi, exposed the Mafia organization to the American public.

Many histories have since been written about the Mafia. Frank Palmeri says some are accurate and some are not. He wanted to report what he knew about the Mafia's decline since 1980. He wanted to offer his own insights into the organization. This is his history.

#

DOMINOES

C all me the last of my kind. I'm a made man. Swore the blood oath, omertà, and never looked back when I became a member of one of the Five Families in the Mafia. I came around when bosses, captains, and soldiers were real men, not like the rats we have today who earn their money then betray their friends when the feds make the going tough.

I've been in "the life" most of my life. My name is Frank Palmeri. Palmeri is not my real name because even though I make my living now by legitimate means, I'm still a member of the Mafia. I always will be. As I said, I swore the oath. The Mafia is more than a crime organization; it's the life you live. I served time because of a wire-wearing rat. Now I'm writing this book and sharing information about a secret organization that is no longer secret because the rats have spilled everything.

So you understand, this book is not written by an informant who wants to look good now that he has cooperated with the government. I never cooperated. I served my time like a man. It's not written by someone in law enforcement who infiltrated one of the Five Families in New York like that Donnie Brasco, the undercover FBI agent who served as an associate of the Bonanno Family—we called them the Banana Family—for six years in the late 1970s and early '80s. That book was bullshit. The FBI had infiltrated the weakest family and the weakest group in the family.

This book is written by me, a real wiseguy who was around during the last forty years when the feds started using RICO (the 1970 Racketeer Influenced and Corrupt Organization Act) in 1981 to break the Mafia. I was around when John Gotti became boss, something that should never have happened because, with all due respect, John didn't have what it took to be a boss. "Our Thing," *Costa Nostra*, started to go bad when one wiseguy after another turned rat. When they started cooperating, the feds began to clear members of the Five Families off the streets of New York. It was like watching dominoes getting knocked over. Hell, now it seems like there are more guys in witness protection than there are working the streets.

The worst rat, the one that may have sealed the fate of the mob's organization, is Joe Massino, the former boss of the Bonnano Family. He turned against his own men. Then, in a travesty of justice, he got released on time served, which wasn't much for someone who killed, or had ordered killed, many people. He got to keep much of his money while other wiseguys who were convicted had to give up their earnings.

One of the rules of being the boss of a family is to make sure your captains and soldiers fear you. They must know you are decisive and that you will punish them for not following the rules. The second rule is to make sure they respect you because you are decisive, fair, and loyal. Fear and respect are the only way to keep order and get people to follow your lead.

But after Massino cooperated with the government, why would anybody want to be loyal to a boss? Why would a wiseguy follow orders when there's a real chance the boss will turn him in for murders and crimes he ordered the guy to do?

Massino and all the rats may have broken the Mafia; at least the Mafia I knew when there were bosses like Carlo Gambino and Vincent "Chin" Gigante. They were loyal to their soldiers but demanded respect, because men feared what could happen to them if they did not live up to the Mafia code.

I've seen firsthand most of what's happened to the Mafia during the last three decades, and while I wasn't at all the meetings of the bosses, I was told by those who were there what was discussed. Now, I have a story to tell. This book is a history of the last forty years of the Mafia. It's largely about the Gambino Family and its big bosses: Paul Castellano, John Gotti, and Sammy Gravano. They rose fast, fell hard, and brought down a lot of people with them. This book is about how that family went from honor and respect to no honor. It became all about the money and greed. Their downfalls were the dominoes that started knocking out the mob.

Every action and reaction by Castellano, Gotti, and Gravano was about money. In John's case it was also about ego. I'll tell you the mistakes those bosses made and the motives behind the moves they made that ultimately lead to death (Castellano), imprisonment for life (Gotti), and decision to turn rat (Gravano).

Not everyone can run a mob family. It isn't easy. You have to think like a fox and have the heart of a lion. It doesn't mean you use killing as an answer to everything like Gotti and Gravano did. To run a mob family, you have to be a great thinker and always one step ahead of your men. Never get too comfortable as the boss; never think no one will come at you because you are the boss. Paul Castellano did. He let his guard down, and they killed him because of it.

4

In this book, I will share with you stories never before told of how the Mafia was and what it took to be a successful mob boss. I will tell you what went wrong. And lastly, I will tell you why you shouldn't go into the life.

The Mafia, and in particular the Five Families, have seen better days, but make no mistake—the mob may be down, but it's certainly not out. How it survives, if it survives—and I have my doubts that it will—remains to be seen.

Chapter Two

King of Rats

Let me start with a guy who did tremendous damage to the mob in the late 1990s. He was a Mafia wannabe, Michael "Cookie" D'Urso. He's one of those guys in the life who becomes a rat with a multitude of excuses for why he was in the Mafia. He uses excuses to make himself appear more sympathetic and to shine a more favorable light on his situation. A rat complains he was treated poorly in the Mafia even though he gave his entire life and work to the mob.

D'Urso didn't have what it took to be a member of the Genovese Family. He did nothing for that family, or any other family, to warrant induction into, or even association with, a family. He started his life in crime in Queens with the Giannini crew, a violent gang loosely connected to the Mafia. This

6

crew had about ten members who had no regard for any rules. They operated outside the mob. They used and sold drugs.

Drug dealing had been banned by the Mafia since the 1960s. Although there have been numerous cases of made men dealing because of the lucrative profits, it was nonetheless banned. This crew did what they did because of the money and their drug habits. They knew that if they were ever to be associated with or inducted into a family, the drug dealing and drug lifestyle would have to stop. But since they were not officially under a family, they did what they did.

One of the Giannini trademarks was to find a drug dealer selling a significant amount of drugs and making a significant amount of money. They would rob him of both and kill him. They often shook down other drug dealers, making them pay protection money to continue to operate. The Giannini crew was feared because of their reputation for killing for the slightest reason or no reason whatsoever. So, drug dealers paid.

Around 1993, through an intermediary, D'Urso borrowed $30,000 on the point system from a made member of the Gambino Family, Pasquale "Patsy" Conte. When D'Urso could not maintain the $600 per week payments, Patsy became fed up and began to research D'Urso. He discovered that D'Urso was a drug-using lowlife with no regard and no respect for anyone. Patsy no longer cared about the money, which is one of the biggest reasons anyone enters the life. He now wanted D'Urso dead.

When D'Urso found out about the price on his head, he ran to his cousin, Sabatino "Tino" Lombardi. At the time, Tino was the maître d' at a popular mob-frequented restaurant located in Little Italy. The restaurant stood on Grand Street between Mott and Mulberry streets. It was called Ruggiero's.

This restaurant was owned by a Genovese wiseguy, Joseph Zito. Zito's partner in crime at the time was Salvatore "Sammy Meatballs" Aparo. Tino loved his cousin, Cookie, and did not want to see anything happen to him. He put himself on the line to get help from the mobsters he worked for.

Tino was well liked and respected by Zito and Sammy, so they arranged a meeting with Patsy Conte to discuss the D'Urso situation. During the meeting, Patsy said he did not want the money owed to him, he wanted D'Urso killed. He felt nothing good could ever come from the kid. He thought D'Urso was nothing but slime.

But Zito and Sammy believed everything Tino told them were the good qualities of D'Urso. They continued to go to bat for him. It took several meetings for Zito and Sammy to finally convince Patsy to take the money owed to him as a favor to them. In mob circles you bend and do favors. So, Patsy gave in—as a favor—and said, "Ok, you can have this cancer."

From that moment on, D'Urso owed the $30,000 to Zito and Sammy. To guarantee their money and to make a profit on saving his life, they put him to work doing several mob activities. Tino joined his cousin in earning for Zito and Sammy by loan-sharking, getting money at a low rate, and pushing it on the street at a high rate. They also sold swag or stolen goods, ran a credit card fraud business, a gambling club, and a sports betting operation. D'Urso was now officially an associate of the Genovese Family, protected by Zito and Sammy.

One of the clubs they opened was the San Giuseppe Social Club on Graham Avenue in East Williamsburg, Brooklyn, near the Brooklyn-Queens Expressway. The club was their base of operation every evening. During the day they always made appearances in Little Italy by hanging out in Ruggiero's.

On occasion, Carmine "Carmine Pizza" Polito would come into Ruggiero's to borrow money from Sammy. Carmine's family owned many successful pizza restaurants, and he owned one himself. He was a well-liked, honorable man known by all associates and wiseguys. Carmine absolutely loved to gamble. Sports betting and high-stakes card games were his favorites. Carmine, like many gamblers, would often gamble more than he could afford. So, on occasion, he would get into serious trouble owing more than he had. He would borrow on a point system to make his gambling debts good.

Now, Carmine had a gambling partner, Mario "The Baker" Fortunato. One of the clubs Mario and Carmine frequented to gamble was the social club owned by Genovese wiseguy Tommy Giggoli on Mulberry Street between Grant and Broom streets. Every Monday they played cards there. Tino and D'Urso would occasionally pop in to play cards. Although they would see Carmine in Ruggiero's on occasion, the social club was where they spent time playing cards with Mario and Carmine. They would constantly invite the two gamblers to play at their club in Brooklyn. Tino and D'Urso saw Mario and Carmine as an opportunity to get more action and more profits with card games and sports betting. Eventually, Carmine and Mario became regulars at Tino and D'Urso's San Giuseppe Social Club.

Carmine continued to gamble more than he had and often borrowed money from Sammy. He started out borrowing $10,000 at a time, then $20,000 and up. Now, especially on the streets, you don't go out and start off borrowing $100,000. It's like any credit system. You have to build it up.

Since he frequented Tino and D'Urso's club often, Carmine would make his payments to Sammy by dropping the money off to D'Urso or Tino. Even when he had to pay back the principal of $10,000 or $20,000, Carmine would give it to them, knowing it would go to Sammy. Soon enough, Carmine was well over his head and into Sammy for $60,000. He honorably made the vig or interest payments every week, often through D'Urso and Tino at the club.

Besides his family's pizza businesses, Carmine also had a small crew of thieves whose favorite jobs were armored car heists, which would eventually land Carmine in prison. One day Carmine apparently made a score, whether from a heist or a lucky streak of gambling, and suddenly he had the money to repay his loan with Sammy.

So, Carmine shows up at the San Giuseppe Social Club with $60,000 to pay off Sammy and some extra cash to gamble. He gave the $60,000 to D'Urso and Tino, but they begged Carmine not to tell Sammy he had made the payoff because they wanted to use the money. They promised Carmine they would pay the vig. Unbeknownst to Sammy, Tino and D'Urso had spent most of the money they were supposed to have had out on the street for him. They wanted to use the $60,000 and keep it under Carmine's name.

Carmine refused to agree to that arrangement. He had owed the money for a while, and he wanted his slate clean. If something happened to Tino or D'Urso, he would still be responsible for repaying the money. Carmine insisted that he would tell Sammy personally the next day that he'd paid off the loan. With the cash he had left over, Carmine sat down to play cards as he normally did, unconcerned that Tino and D'Urso were upset that he wouldn't agree to their deal. D'Urso and Tino took the $60,000 upstairs to D'Urso's aunt for safekeeping.

Approximately two hours later, a gunman wearing a mask entered the club. He was supposedly there to rob everyone, but instead he went directly toward Carmine, who realized it was a set up and fled. As Carmine was jumping through the window, the gunman got one shot off and hit him in the leg. The gunman then proceeded to take everyone's cash and exit the club.

The next day, Tino and D'Urso went to Mulberry Street, gave Sammy the $60,000 from Carmine, and informed him of the robbery. Carmine was sent for by Sammy. They discussed what had happened.

Sammy was sorry Carmine was shot. Supposedly, Sammy was going to investigate to bring the gunman to justice, but nothing ever came of it. In their discussion, Carmine, being a stand-up guy, never told Sammy about Tino and D'Urso wanting to keep the $60,000. Things went back to business as usual.

Carmine returned to playing cards shortly afterward at the San Giuseppe Social Club. Since the shooting, Mario "the Baker" was back playing cards there as well. It seemed as though everything was forgotten, and the shooting was assumed to be a robbery and nothing more. In the meantime, Carmine was plotting to take retribution for what he knew was an attempted hit on him. He recruited John Imbrieco, Anthony Bruno, and Angelo Cerasulo to assist in his revenge.

Over the next year, Carmine and Mario slowly introduced new players to the club. The three-man hit team Carmine had organized for his revenge became regulars at the card games, even frequenting the club when Carmine and Mario were not present. D'Urso and Tino had no idea that Carmine had planned to kill them. On many a night, the group would play well into the morning hours for high stakes and a lot of laughs. Carmine's men also placed big bets, winning and losing with D'Urso and Tino's book. The two cousins were very comfortable with the three men and actually looked forward to playing cards with them.

So, on the night of November 30, 1994, sitting at the table playing cards were "Carmine Pizza" Polito, his partner Mario "The Baker" Fortunate, John Imbrieco, Angelo Cerasulo, Anthony Bruno, Sabatino "Tino" Lombardi, and Michael "Cookie" D'Urso.

The following scene in the club was right out of *The Godfather*: John Imbrieco returned from the bathroom, gun in hand, and opened fire on Tino. As John shot Tino six times, Anthony Bruno stood up and shot D'Urso once in the back of the head. Assuming the two cousins are dead, the five men fled the club.

D'Urso, though, was not dead. He was able to drag himself outside where he reached up, rang his aunt's doorbell, and collapsed, unconscious. His aunt came down from the upstairs apartment screaming and called 911. D'Urso was rushed to the hospital where the surgeons successfully removed the bullet from his head.

Sammy rushed to D'Urso bedside upon news of the shooting. While D'Urso was in the hospital's intensive care unit, Sammy would tell people that Cookie was like a son to him. But could his real concern have been his $150,000 that he thought D'Urso and Tino had out on the street as loans?

As always, it was all about the money.

In the hospital, the doctor told Sammy that D'Urso pulling through like he did was like hitting the Lotto three times in one week.

By the summer of 1995, D'Urso was back on the street. He met with Sammy and confessed that the $150,000 was actually not on the street, but spent. He blamed it on Tino, his cousin, who was dead and could not defend himself.

D'Urso told Sammy that Tino had been an out-of-control gambler and had gambled the $150,000 away. D'Urso said he couldn't stop Tino and didn't want him to get into trouble. That was his reason, he told Sammy, for not telling the truth. D'Urso then promised to repay the $150,000 over time.

Sammy decided to give D'Urso fresh money to open another sports sheet with the agreement that as D'Urso earned from the fresh money he would pay down his $150,000 debt.

During his meeting with Sammy, D'Urso requested retribution for the murder of Tino and the attempt on his life. Sammy informs D'Urso that, regardless of the reasons, wiseguys did not just go out and kill people. No matter who you are in the Genovese Family, you have to first get an okay from everyone else before you kill someone.

Sammy was just a soldier in the Genovese Family. As a soldier he could not just reach out and directly communicate with the bosses. A soldier must bring any type of serious request, or dispute, to his captain. The captain would then make a decision and come up with a resolution before bringing it to the attention of a boss.

However, when there's a request to take someone's life, it is not the captain's place to make the decision. It must go to the boss. Sammy's captain was Rosario "Rossi" Gangi, who, after only hearing D'Urso's version of events and trusting Sammy, decided there was merit to the request. Gangi believed that retribution should be taken. No one went after an associate without severe consequences. Therefore, Gangi was granted a meeting with Frank "Farby" Serpico (no relation to the former New York City Policeman Frank Serpico), who was the acting boss at the time while the real bosses were in prison.

The Genovese Family, unlike the other families, will thoroughly investigate any murder and requests for vengeance before making a final decision. They do not just give the green light on a killing at the drop of a hat. They have a high respect for life. That is why they are the most successful and strongest of the families. They don't just kill.

When Gangi met with Farby, the boss already knew about the incident. He had investigated the back stories to the killing and the attempt on D'Urso's life. He was aware that D'Urso and Tino attempted to kill Carmine to keep the $60,000. He knew the killing of Tino and the attempt on D'Urso's life was payback for something that D'Urso initiated. So, Farby gave the order that no one was to be killed and the incident was to be forgotten.

Sammy was upset by Farby's order because he'd just given D'Urso fresh money, plus D'Urso owed him $150,000. Sammy did not want to make D'Urso bitter toward him over Farby's decision, so he told D'Urso that in time he would put him in for membership. Membership meant that he would become a made member of the Genovese Family. Once D'Urso was made, he could again request to kill Carmine.

D'Urso was beyond upset. But when an order comes from the top it's final and nothing can be, nor should be, done to countermand it. But Sammy was, with all due respect, not so bright. He still believed D'Urso and hadn't figured out that D'Urso was actually trying to rob him of the $60,000 from Carmine.

Sammy's concern should have been to get his money back from D'Urso, not involve himself in criminal activities with other family members. Keeping D'Urso involved and promising to get him made may have been Sammy's way of making sure that he was repaid his $150,000 sooner rather than later.

Sammy believed D'Urso had earning potential, which a wiser man would not have believed. A wiser man would not have trusted D'Urso, no matter how great his earning potential, because D'Urso was not honorable. He was trouble. Furthermore, Sammy should have realized that all the incidents—the attempt on Carmine's life, the death of Tino, the attempt on D'Urso's life, and the $150,000 D'Urso and Tino blew—combined with the original Patsy Conte situation indicated that D'Urso was no good.

Patsy wanted D'Urso dead instead of having his $30,000 returned, but Sammy allowed D'Urso to continue to operate under him. D'Urso had a sports sheet. He received a percentage of the losses of every gambler he introduced. Anyone on his sheet who happened to lose, D'Urso was responsible to collect. If they won, he was responsible to pay.

The system worked on the black and red balances. For example, at the end of the week, if players had more losses, then his sheet would be $20,000 in the black and he would receive half, $10,000. If players had a winning week, then his sheet would be $20,000 in the red, and he would not receive anything. Before he could earn anything else in the following weeks, he had to recoup the $20,000 to get out of the red. Then, whatever went into the black, he would again receive 50 percent.

As I said, D'Urso was trouble, and he would soon bring plenty of trouble to the Genovese Family. D'Urso had a gambler on his sports sheet. The man lived in Queens. Every week, D'Urso would visit him, either with a payment for him from winnings or to collect from him for losses. Each visit, he would brag to the guy that he was going to become a made man soon. He repeated several times that he was going to be the youngest made wiseguy in the Genovese Family. This, of course, should never be said to anyone, especially someone who is not directly involved with organized crime. In the Mafia, one of the biggest rules is supposed to be secrecy. The success of any secret organization requires secrecy.

One week, the man from Queens lost about $36,000. That amount happened to be well over what he could afford to pay. He was cut off from D'Urso's sheet and not allowed to place anymore bets. D'Urso continued to visit the guy for the money owed, but the man's stories and excuses began to anger him. He wanted his money and no more excuses. D'Urso's began to threaten the guy with violence and pain.

The Queens man was unable to come up with the money immediately and needed more time to pay. He was fearful for his life because of D'Urso's bragging about becoming a wiseguy. So, the guy ran to a friend. This friend knew Farby Serpico, the acting boss of the Genovese Family. Farby would never talk on the phone with anyone, but in that situation he broke his rule because it was made clear to him that D'Urso was going to hurt the Queens man. Farby was well aware of D'Urso's name from D'Urso's previous request to kill Carmine.

Farby called D'Urso and said, "You don't know who I am, but I am very good friends with your uncle Sammy Meatballs." Leave the fellah in Queens alone until I can see Sammy." D'Urso responded violently. "I want my fucking money!" Farby, again patiently, said, "Don't go near those people. I will reach out to Sammy tomorrow." Then Farby ended the conversation by hanging up.

When any person in the know—whether a made member, an associate, a knock around guy, or any one from the street—gets a phone call like that, they should investigate before taking action. Regardless, whether it's a call from a real wiseguy or not, a person should take caution. D'Urso should have gone straight to Sammy to inform him about the call. Instead, he went directly to Queens.

D'Urso rang the bell. The man's wife answered the door. D'Urso violently shoved her aside, and then grabbed the man. He held a knife to his throat and yelled, "I don't give a fuck who you know. I want my fucking money! I'm coming back on Monday! And if you don't have my fucking money, I'm cutting your fucking throat!" This was on a Saturday.

As soon as D'Urso left, the man from Queens called his friend, all shaken up. The man told the friend what happened and said D'Urso obviously didn't care about the boss in the Genovese Family because he was definitely coming back on Monday to kill him. The friend, shocked, quickly made the necessary calls.

The news immediately reached Farby, who was now furious. Farby knew that he was probably too irate at that moment to make a wise decision. That very night, he reached out to one of his respected captains from Brooklyn, Alan Longo. Longo is known for diplomacy and his skill for making peace and having everyone feel they won in any sit down situation. Farby directed Longo to get Sammy and Gangi. He wanted a meeting first thing Sunday morning in the Bronx.

Early Sunday, the day after D'Urso attacked the man in Queens, Longo picked up Sammy and Gangi on Cropsey Avenue in Brooklyn. They headed to the meeting in Longo's Cadillac. On the way, Sammy nervously asked Longo what the meeting was about. Guys in the life know when they get sent for, especially that quick, it's probably not good for them or their interests. Longo told him he hadn't a clue. Farby was very upset, Longo said. "Do any of your guys have a problem?" Longo knew it couldn't have been anything Sammy or Gangi had done.

They arrived in the Bronx and were greeted by one of Farby's men on White Plains Road. They proceeded to follow the man in Longo's vehicle to a restaurant. Of course, being early in the morning on a Sunday the restaurant was closed. They entered the restaurant where a room had been set up just for the meeting. Farby sat waiting for them. They could see the blood boiling under his skin.

The first words out of Farby's mouth were, "Who the fuck does this D'Urso think he is?" He pointed at Sammy. "This fucking kid can't have any respect for you!"

Sammy, who had no idea what had happened, didn't respond. He knew better. He patiently listened as Farby told everyone in the room what had happened, and the phone call he'd made. Then he pointed at Sammy and said, "Did you know all of this was going on?"

"No, I didn't know anything about it," Sammy said quickly.

Sammy and Gangi apologized repeatedly to Farby while promising that D'Urso would never go back to the man's house again. They promised they would handle the situation. "We'll make sure nothing like this ever happens again," they told Farby.

But Farby was still irate. "I mentioned your name on the phone to him, Sammy, and he goes back and puts a knife to this guy's neck. Say it was Pete Gotti on the other end of the phone, or Joe Massino, the boss of the Bonanno Family. What would happen to him then?"

Farby's point was that in the other families, a situation like that didn't warrant a sit down. The offending, non-made member would be automatically killed. The Genovese Family has more respect and compassion for human life, but Farby's anger at D'Urso's disrespect enraged him. Farby looked at Longo and said, "What would you do in this situation if this happened to you?"

Longo knew how angry Farby was and that he was close to ordering D'Urso killed. He knew Farby needed time to cool off. Longo also respected Sammy and Gangi as men of their words. They had been going to bat for the kid, and Longo didn't want to see anything happen. Longo answered. "Our two friends have been around this life for a good thirty years. I would respect their wishes and let them handle it."

That took a little steam out of him. Farby said, "I gotta think about this. We'll meet again in a couple of days." On the way back to Brooklyn, Gangi told Sammy, "Tell D'Urso to leave the man from Queens alone. Tell him to lay low until we straighten this all out."

Sammy did not want to see anything happen to D'Urso, who owed him $150,000 plus the fresh money Sammy had given him for the street. Sammy sent for D'Urso immediately. They met at Florio's Restaurant on Mulberry and Grant streets in Little Italy. They took a walk outside and Sammy said, "Are you losing your fucking mind?"

D'Urso, not knowing there had been a sit down, said, "What do ya mean?"

Sammy said, "The guy that spoke to you on the phone and told you he would get in touch with me was Farby."

"What the fuck do I know who was on the phone?" D'Urso said.

"What the fuck is the difference of who's on the phone?" Sammy said. "You were supposed to come and check with me as soon as you heard my name; not go back to the guy with a knife. Now this guy, Farby, is looking to kill you. We have to go back and meet again over this. You better lay low until it's over."

Three days later, Farby sent for Sammy and Gangi. Gangi, thinking ahead, decided to bring Joe Zito, Sammy's partner, to the meeting. Normally, in any situation when a man is called for, you never bring anyone, made man or not, who wasn't specifically called for. However, Zito had a close relationship with Farby and Gangi was banking on that soothing Farby's anger. When they arrived at the meeting, Farby was happy to see Zito and embraced him. Farby addressed the issue right away. D'Urso was banished from New York City. He would never be allowed to become a made man, and he was never to collect on the Queens gambler's debt.

"I want this kid out of New York," Farby said. "I better never see this kid's name on a list and as far as the debt this guy owes, that's dead." No one else had to speak. The decision was made. The meeting was over.

If Sammy had been smart he would have excluded D'Urso from further activities and made him leave New York. Instead, D'Urso went to Florida, but kept returning under the radar with Sammy's consent. Sammy overlooked how that was an act of disrespect to Farby. Soon after the sit down where Farby said he wanted D'Urso out of New York for good, D'Urso was back in his place in Williamsburg, Brooklyn.

Early one morning in 1998, the FBI knocked down D'Urso's door and placed him under arrest. They charged him with involvement in a murder. It was alleged that he furnished the gun that helped kill John Borelli in 1996. The moment they started to read him his rights, he asked for Agent Mike Campi, now retired but then the head of the FBI's Genovese Squad of the Organized Crime Task Force.

D'Urso was aware of the agent because Campi would walk right into Florio's Restaurant from time to time and say to Sammy, "Hello, Sammy. Pretty soon your number is gonna come up," or "We gotcha, it's only a matter of time."

One night, Campi entered the social club where the regular Monday night card games are held. He went directly to Tommy Giggoli, a made member of the Genovese Family and owner of the club. He dropped a number of photos onto the table in front of him. As Campi spread out the photos he asked, "What do you know about these men?"

Tommy shrugged his shoulders and said, "They are just a bunch of old men who come in here to play cards."

Campi laughed and pointed at certain photos. "These three guys are bank robbers, these couple of guys are bookmakers, and all of these guys are murderers; yeah, just old men playing cards." He collected the photos with a big smile, as if he was letting Giggoli know that everyone was going down. As he left, he said, "I'll be seeing you real soon."

When Campi showed up at D'Urso's home that morning, he was wearing that smile because D'Urso had been around Sammy, Pete "Petey Red" DiChiara, Sammy's son, Vinny, Zito, and a bunch of other wiseguys. Campi would have someone wear a wire in Florio's so he could collar the very men that he had been after. D'Urso did not disappoint him.

Sammy would never get back the $150,000 D'Urso owed him.

I would later learn that the 1998 arrest of D'Urso was prearranged by the FBI because D'Urso had decided to become a government informant. The information he provided during the next three years caused one of many upheavals in the Mafia over the last three decades.

While a growing number of Mafia members have become informants since the 1970s, a federal prosecutor called D'Urso's work of wearing a wire and collecting information "remarkable and historic." It led to the arrests and convictions of more than seventy members of the Genovese Family, including the late boss, Vincent "Chin" Gigante, acting boss Dominick "Quiet Dom" Cirillo, and two underbosses.

Sammy, Zito, DiChiara, Longo, Gangi, and Farby were among the initial forty-five of the seventy Genovese Family members who were arrested and convicted based on the wire-recorded evidence provided by D'Urso. Except for Farby, who died of natural causes before he was sentenced, all these men have served their time and been released from prison. D'Urso did not serve time for his role in the murder of John Borelli. He and his wife live under the federal witness protection program.

No one just turns rat. Nobody just starts telling on their friends. When someone cooperates with the feds it's because they are born that way. It just takes something to bring it out of them, like getting arrested with the chance of going to prison.

There are no excuses for being a rat, but informants would like people to believe there are. Guys talk and say things like, "While I was in prison my friend fucked my wife," or "While I was locked up no one sent me money," or "While I was locked up they demoted me." All these excuses are bullshit. A real man would never roll over. He would die first.

Chapter Three

ANASTASIA TO GOTTI

When the Five Families and the Commission were created in New York City in the early 1930s, the American Mafia was all about honor, respect, and, especially, honor. Unfortunately, after so many years, it became all about money.

In 1931, Lucky Luciano named Vincent Mangano the first boss of what would later be named the Gambino Family. Albert Anastasia was Mangano's underboss, the second in command. At the time, Carlo Gambino was just a captain.

A captain has soldiers, made men, under him. If a soldier has a problem with another soldier in his family or with another family, and he can't settle it on his own, the soldier goes to his captain. If the captain can't settle the problem, he goes to his underboss. Only if his underboss thinks it's necessary does the underboss bring the problem to the boss. Back in the early days, a soldier never met with the boss.

Anastasia wasn't happy about being the number two man. He wanted the top spot. So, one day in 1951, Mangano disappeared. Anastasia took over the family. He had the support of most of the captains. But Mangano's brother, Philip, a made man in the family, started to ask questions about Vincent's disappearance. So, Philip was shot to death. Anastasia was the official boss and nobody said a word.

Anastasia broke a rule and got away with it. You just don't go and kill an official boss. You have to go in front of all the other bosses on the Commission and get an okay. But out of fear of another war, the Commission and everyone else went along with what happened. They shouldn't have because it would eventually undermine the organization that made the Mafia work.

Anastasia, who now had the Brooklyn waterfront under his control and ruled with an iron fist, made Carlo Gambino his underboss.

Anastasia loved the nightlife and loved to gamble. Horses were his favorite. When problems reached him, he knew only one solution: kill the guy. And when his gambling got out of control, he started taking money off his men and selling membership into the family. These were not the actions of a good boss, particularly if one wanted his men's loyalty.

Meanwhile, Luciano, the boss of the later-to-be-named Genovese Family, which became the biggest mob family with the most members and with the most money coming in of any of the Five Families, had been deported to Italy four years earlier in 1947.

Luciano's underboss, Vito Genovese, was on the run from the law because of a murder charge. So Luciano left his consigliere, Frank Costello, as the acting boss. Costello wasn't about muscle. He was one of the biggest earners in the Mafia. He also had a lot of connections in New York City Hall.

Costello and Anastasia became close, but they weren't doing well as bosses. At one point, Costello wasn't servicing his captains. They couldn't get to see him. Also, word was getting around about Anastasia selling membership into his family.

Genovese came out of hiding after a couple of witnesses that could testify against him disappeared. He took in everything that was going on between Costello and Anastasia, then waited and plotted for almost ten years.

Then, on the morning of October 25, 1957, when Anastasia was getting his scheduled shave at the Park Sheraton Hotel, a couple of Genovese's top gunmen showed up and killed Anastasia as he sat in the barber's chair.

Through the years there were stories that Genovese used the Gallo brothers from Brooklyn or out-of-town gunmen to kill Anastasia. But this was not true. Genovese had an army, and he had his most trusted men to do the hit.

Genovese knew that if the hit hadn't been done right and Anastasia had lived, a war between Anastasia and Genovese would have started. So you can bet Genovese used his own men. At the same time Anastasia was being hit, Genovese sent Vincent "Chin" Gigante out to kill Costello.

Chin didn't get him. As Chin walked up behind Costello, he said, "This is for you, Frank," just before firing his gun. When Costello turned to see who was talking to him, the bullet grazed his head. Chin fled immediately after the shooting, thinking that he had killed Costello. Scared, Costello dropped out of sight.

With those two hits, Genovese became the most powerful boss in the country, which opened the door for Carlo Gambino to become boss of his family. With Genovese's blessing, Gambino picked Aniello "Mr. O'Neil" Dellacroce as his underboss and Joe N. Gallo as his consigliere. He made his brother-in-law, Paul Castellano, a captain in the family.

Just the fact that Gambino was the new boss of the family gave all the captains and soldiers a relaxed feeling. The men weren't afraid of getting killed for nothing as they were with Anastasia as boss.

Gambino picked moneymaking captains. His underboss, Dellacroce, had all the tough guys under him. If something had to be taken care of, Dellacroce got the job done. Dellacroce was a guy who liked the nightlife and loved his club, the Ravenite on Mulberry Street, where he would go most afternoons to play cards.

Gambino, on the other hand, was reserved. He never went to prison because he kept things low key. That's how he lasted as boss from 1957 to 1976.

When Gambino's nephew, Emmanuel, was kidnapped and killed in 1973, the Gambino Family found out the killer was an Irish guy from Staten Island, James McBratney. Gambino gave the job to his underboss, Dellacroce, who gave the hit to one of his captains, Carmine "Charley Wagons" Fatico.

Fatico, who had a tough crew under him, assigned the job to three guys: John Gotti, Angelo Ruggiero, and Ralph "Ralphie Wigs" Galione. They went to a bar in Staten Island to take care of McBratney. The plan was to get McBratney outside. But when the trio walked into the bar, their plan didn't look like it would work. So, Galione just opened fire. He shot McBratney three times and killed him.

Gotti and Ruggiero were upset with Galione and killed him for what he did. Gotti, Ruggiero, and Galione were not made men at the time. Neither the Gambinos nor any other crime family was making new members. The books had been closed since the killing of Anastasia in '57.

In 1976, Gambino became very ill and willed the family in front of Dellacroce and Joe N. Gallo to his brother-in-law, Paul Castellano. It doesn't always work out that way, but when Gambino died of a heart attack later that year, Castellano became boss.

Castellano, already well off, didn't need a dime. He should have let Dellacroce become head of the family, but Castellano was greedy and wanted the top spot. He kept Mr. O'Neil, as Dellacroce was often called, as underboss, and Joe N. Gallo as consigliere.

During the same year of Gambino's death, the books opened for membership. The Genovese Family was against making new members, but with Gambino's passing and Castellano as the new boss, it was decided to open the books.

Castellano put in the first members, Tommy Bilotti and Frankie DeCicco. Mr. O'Neil's crew put in John Gotti and Angelo Ruggiero. Many others were made from 1976 through 1977.

Around 1978, Gotti's captain, Danny Fatico, the brother of Carmine Fatico, became ill. His health started to fail. Gotti became acting captain of the Fatico crew. Gotti did all the running around for Fatico and loved it. Gotti loved the street life. He lived it every day.

John knew most of the other families' members and most of them liked John. Gotti was out eating and drinking most nights. He loved the nightlife and could handle it, too. One of his favorite drinks was a martini. He could put them away. We would say, "John, how do you drink all those martinis and still get up and walk?" He would say, "Some people make the martinis wrestle them; I wrestle the martinis."

After hours of eating and drinking in the restaurants, John would go to the disco and drink all night. He also had another habit—gambling, which he was out of control with. He loved football, baseball, and horses. He was like every other hard-luck gambler. One thing about gambling that you can't beat is that nobody wins in the end. The only people that win all the time are the bookmakers. So John was always into the loan sharks paying vig. One of John's favorite sayings was, "If a guy don't drink and gamble, watch him."

Gotti was good with his hands. He knew how to fight. He had no problem knocking someone out with a punch. One night he was in Abe's Steakhouse on 73rd Street and 3rd Avenue in Manhattan. He and a couple of his guys were at the bar having drinks before dinner. There was this big guy drinking next to him and every minute or so he would move into John and push all of them down the bar into the corner. John finally said to the guy, "Hey, pal, can you give us some room?" The answer wasn't polite. John knocked the guy out with one punch, but hurt his hand. He had to keep it bandaged for a while.

Another time John and one of his guys were at a disco in Brooklyn. The friend left to go to the bathroom to piss. While in the bathroom standing at the urinal, a guy next to him who was drunk said, "Hey, fellow, I'd like to pee on you." The friend told John what happened and said, "I'm going to beat the shit out of this guy." John, who was much tougher than his friend, said, "I got this." The drunk guy walked out of the disco, and John, who was waiting outside, said to the guy, "Hey, pal, how you doing?" Then he proceeded to beat the shit out of him.

A funny story about John: He was on his way to Staten Island for a meeting at Mr. O' Neil's house one night. It was raining lightly outside and while driving over the bridge, he saw an accident ahead. He tried to slow down, but ended up tapping into one of the cars involved in the accident. One of the guys at the accident scene told John to step out of his car. It was raining and John was dressed up, so John told the guy, "No." The guy proceeded to hit John in the face with a police slapjack. John got out of his car and started hitting the guy. Before he knew it, there were about six cops on him. John said later it was like the Keystone Cops; the cops were hitting each other more than they were hitting him. The guy who hit John with the slapjack ended up being a cop.

Now John was at the station house in Staten Island and before he knew it, Frank DeCicco and Angelo Ruggiero showed up. They told the cops, "You are not locking him up." A police sergeant said, "Look what he did to my uniform. And he also said he was going to kill my wife and kids." John ended up getting out with only a desk summons.

That was John Gotti. He thought with his fists instead of his brains.

Chapter Four

NEITHER FOX NOR LION

Paul Castellano was a smart business man. But a boss of a Mafia family needs to think like a fox and have the heart of a lion. Paul had neither. A boss needs to keep his men happy, and make them earn just enough so they don't turn on him. Tommy Bilotti was Paul's man. Paul took care of Tommy and Tommy only.

For example, a captain who ran the docks in Brooklyn for Paul came to him one day with $100,000 that he had made off the docks. Paul took his half as the boss, but out of the captain's $50,000 he gave Bilotti $25,000. The captain only received $25,000 out of the $100,000 he had scored on his own. The captain was not happy. Paul should've taken care of Bilotti from his end, not the captain's, but that was Paul's greed.

Paul made Bilotti and Frankie DeCicco captains in the Gambino Family, but he always talked down to DeCicco. DeCicco was a big gambler and always in trouble, but he held his own. Paul would one day come to regret his mistreatment of DeCicco.

One day, DeCicco, Joe Sis, also a made man in the Gambino Family, and Johnny Boy, who was not a made member, came away from a heist with $1.5 million. They split it three ways, $500,000 among each of them. DeCicco took $5,000 from Joe Sis and $5,000 from Johnny Boy. He put in $10,000 of his own and bought Paul a $20,000 Rolex watch.

When DeCicco presented the watch, Paul's response was, "What's this for?"

DeCicco said, "Me, Joe Sis, and Johnny Boy made a score."

"How much?" Paul asked.

"A million and a half," DeCicco responded.

Paul said, "Here, take the watch back and bring me fifty thousand dollars each."

DeCicco, Joe, and Johnny were sick about it, but they had to come up with the money.

When there's a racket in the family, the boss can take 50 percent. But when made men put their lives on the line to go on a score, the boss has nothing coming. So the Rolex watch was a good gesture by the three of them, but there was the greed again.

DeCicco had no love for his boss.

The Commission, made up of the bosses of the Five Families, would meet every once in a while to solve problems. At one meeting, Paul was there for his family, Vincent "Chin" Gigante for the Genovese Family, Tony "Ducks" Corallo for the Lucchese Family, and Tom DiBella for the Colombos. The Bonanno's boss was in prison and there was a split in the family at the time.

A Bonanno caporegime, Alphonse "Sonny Red" Indelicato, was at the meeting and told the bosses, "Pretty soon, we are going to war." Paul was at the head and replied, "I think a war is not a good idea." But Sonny Red insisted and said, "But Paul, you don't understand." Paul tried to be nice and make Sonny Red understand how a war in the Bonanno Family affected all the other families. But Sonny Red again said, "Please, Paul, you don't understand." Then Chin Gigante said, "Excuse me, Paul," then turned to Sonny Red and advised, "You don't understand; if you go to war we will kill all of you. End of story." The Genovese Family didn't put up with too much bullshit.

Drugs were supposed to be outlawed in the Five Families in New York, but sometimes wiseguys didn't listen. There's too much money in drugs. At one of the

Commission meetings, the Genovese boss, Fat Tony Salerno, and Paul took a stand. Together they barred drugs. Fat Tony warned the families, "If you don't clean up your houses, we will."

When you became a made man there were three rules that would get you killed if you didn't follow them: 1. No drugs, 2. No bombs, 3. No stocks or bonds. All of these activities would bring in the feds, and the bosses didn't want that. But it's hard to tell the boss of another family how to run his family.

Fat Tony and Paul were worried that if the other families were into drugs, sooner or later the heat would reach them. The only family that really enforced the no-drug rule was the Genovese Family. The bosses sent word to all the captains—who were required to pass the word to their soldiers—that they didn't want them to do business with anyone in the drug business. That meant no gambling, no lending money—nothing. "It's up to you," the bosses said, "because if you bring us heat you will get killed."

Paul had a couple of captains that were really close to him: James "Jimmy Brown" Failla, who handled all the private sanitation in Manhattan, and Salvatore "Toddo" Aurello, a millionaire businessman. Then there was Carmine Lamdoza, who had been around making money as long as Carlo Gambino. But one captain was loyal to Paul, Anthony "Nino" Gaggi, a big loan shark who gave out big money for weekly vigs.

Nino's crew was Paul's muscle. One of Nino's soldiers was Roy DeMeo. Roy had a tough crew of guys, but none of them were made men, only Roy. They were into stolen cars, but most of their money came from drugs. They also took drugs and killed without an okay from the boss, which was against the rules.

Every week Nino would give Paul a nice fat envelope from the DeMeo crew. For Paul, it was okay because he played it off as money from the stolen car ring, even though most of it came from drugs.

The DeMeo crew operated out of the Gemini Lounge in Canarsie in Brooklyn. They would kill guys in the back of the bar, chop up their bodies, put the parts in black bags, and dump them.

John Gotti became the official captain of the Fatico crew because Carmine Fatico was indicted for loan-sharking and Danny Fatico, Carmine's brother, was too sick to lead the crew. John would answer to the underboss, "Mr. O'Neil" Dellacroce, but was still accountable to Paul.

John's partner and closest friend was Angelo Ruggiero. Angelo's brother, Salvatore "Sal" Ruggiero, was in the heroin business. In 1982, Sal, who was on the run from the government at the time, boarded a Learjet for one of his trips to Florida. The jet crashed over the ocean and everyone was killed. Angelo and a couple of others in John Gotti's crew were in the drug business on the down low.

A big blow soon came to the Gambino Family. Ruggiero, Gene Gotti (one of John's brothers), and two other made men under John were arrested for selling heroin. The case was mostly made around Angelo, whose home and phone were bugged by the FBI. Paul had egg on his face. The indictments were all over the newspapers. Don't forget, Paul made a no-drugs pact with the Genovese Family.

Paul had other problems with Roy DeMeo and his crew. They were out of control. Paul had to do something about their drug dealing, but DeMeo and his crew were also killing people in the Gemini Lounge. According to the FBI, DeMeo and his crew may have killed as many as a hundred people between 1973 and 1983. So, DeMeo was killed. He was found in the trunk of his car. His crew was broken up. Paul, Nino Gaggi, and a couple of others were arrested for the stolen car ring.

Gaggi's nephew, Dominick Montiglio, used to pick up the money from DeMeo and bring it to his uncle Nino. Once in a while he would take the money right to Paul. Montiglio, who was a drug addict, got arrested for extortion and became a rat informant. Based on the information he provided, the Gambino Family's boss and Gaggi were arrested. Paul made bail. Then the fun started.

Once Paul heard there were tapes from Ruggiero's house phone, he wanted copies of the wiretap evidence Ruggiero's lawyer had. Once an individual is arrested and charged, the government shares the evidence with the individual's lawyer. At this same time, Paul's underboss, Mr. O'Neil Dellacroce, was battling cancer. Paul kept asking him for the tapes, but wasn't getting them.

This was another aspect of Paul's failure as a boss. First, Paul wasn't a cop. He was the boss. He should have let the case play out. He should have sent for John Gotti, who was the captain of all those guys, and said, "Let's hope it was a frame and they beat it." But he didn't. He became a joke. It was all over Brooklyn and Manhattan about the tapes. Paul was putting a lot of pressure on Dellacroce to get him the tapes. Gotti and Ruggiero were like sons to Mr. O'Neil, and he would never let anything happen to either of them, but he told them, "Give Paul the tapes."

Paul forgot that John had one of the strongest crews in the Gambino Family. John was never going to let anything happen to his brother Gene or Ruggiero. With Gaggi gone and DeMeo dead, Paul was weak. He should've just cooled down and waited to see how the case played out. He also had his own case to worry about.

43

By then DeCicco hated Paul. DeCicco was another guy who was out every night, eating in restaurants, and going to discos. He often would run into John Gotti. Both had one thing in common: they didn't care for Paul, especially John because of the thing with the tapes.

John and DeCicco started talking about everything and that was when the plan and plot to kill Paul started. Both of those men were tough. Both were hungry, too. You have to remember, John Gotti always had a boss to hold him down so he wouldn't run wild.

First it was his boss Carmine Fatico, who John respected, and then Mr. O'Neil Dellacroce, who John loved like a father. He would need their okay to hit Paul, but Dellacroce was dying of cancer.

Salvatore "Sammy the Bull" Gravano grew up in Bensonhurst. His best friend was Liborio "Louie" Milito. Growing up, Sammy had another friend, Tommy Spero. Tommy's father and Tommy's Uncle "Shorty" Spero were in the Colombo Family. That's who Gravano was around.

Louie Milito was close with a captain in the Gambino Family, Toddo Aurello, who had a club on 17th Avenue in Brooklyn. Even though each man was in a different family, they did a lot of things together. Gravano and Louie were good fighters. Louie was a good earner. Out of the two, Louie was the aggressive earner.

Some of the stories about Gravano are true, but not all of them. Gravano would always make himself the good guy. There was always a reason for what he did. One time, Gravano and Tommy Spero had a falling out over money.

Tommy's uncle Shorty was a close associate of a Colombo captain from downtown Brooklyn. Gravano knew he was in a no-win situation in his argument with Spero, so he went to his friend Louie for help. Louie in turn brought the problem to Toddo Aurello, who was close with his boss, Carlo Gambino.

Gambino asked Joe Colombo, the boss of the Colombo Family, to release Gravano to Toddo. Colombo would never refuse Gambino a favor. And besides, Gravano meant nothing to the Colombo Family. Gravano got released to Toddo and the Gambino Family, thanks to his friend Louie Milito.

Louie and Gravano started to put money out on the street, charging one-and-half percent vig. They got into the construction business and opened their own company. Louie had a used car lot on Staten Island that his wife, Lynda, ran. Louie liked to dress up once in a while and go out with the guys for drinks. Gravano didn't like to dress or drink. He had a farm upstate. He liked to ride horses and hunt.

When the books opened after Gambino died, Louie Milito was made first; Louie made sure Toddo put Gravano in next, which he did. Now Louie and Gravano were made members of the Gambino Family under Captain Toddo Aurello.

When Paul took the top spot in the Gambino Family, he paid a lot of attention to the construction business. The Gambino and Genovese families controlled almost all of the construction in New York. One way or the other, the two families had most of the unions. Concrete was the big earner for all the families. The bosses didn't get involved with the day-to-day business so they put a panel together.

Paul knew about Louie and Gravano's construction business because they would be allowed to go to Paul from time to time, especially since they were both made members of the family. They would ask for help when they had a problem with one of the unions. Paul could see that Louie and Gravano knew what they were doing, so he put the two of them in charge of the family's construction business.

Paul's man with Local 282 was John Cody. When he went to prison, Paul put Bobby Sasso in charge. Louie and Gravano were happy with this arrangement. They also started to report directly to Paul.

The way everyone would always mention John Gotti and Angelo Ruggiero in one breath was how people would refer to Louie Milito and Sammy Gravano because that's how close they were.

Soon enough, John and Sammy would be close.

Chapter Five

LIVE BY THE RULES, DIE BY THE RULES

For secret organizations to function properly and flourish, their members must adhere to rules and protocols. When it comes to organized crime, bosses may need to enforce their rules with murder.

For the Mafia, of course, you won't find these rules written anywhere. They are passed down verbally, from one generation to the next, as each new member is inducted into a "family," better known as becoming a made member.

Unfortunately, for more than thirty years there has been a catastrophic breakdown in rule following in the Mafia. Much of the breakdown and deterioration of the Mafia I used to know, began with John Gotti.

John was a true stand-up guy, tough on the streets, and a good earner for the mob. He was not, however, someone who should have been the boss of the Gambino Family, the second most powerful crime family in America. His downfall was due to his tremendous ego. That led him to make many mistakes; mistakes a boss of a family cannot afford to make.

As everyone in civilian life should know, or will eventually discover, the very best of friends may turn out to be the worst of enemies. This is apparent in the Mafia and should be carefully considered and always remembered.

No one, especially those in the Mafia, should ever put too much trust in a friend. Forget the saying that "it's your best friend who pulls the trigger to kill you." That's not what I'm talking about here.

The biggest reason for the breakdown and betrayal in the Mafia these days is the government informant, the rat. I'm not going to go through an entire history of men who were either associates or made members of the Mafia who became government informants and witnesses, and whose testimonies sent even bosses to prison.

I will, however, illustrate some high-profile witnesses who, living and loving the life, pretended to be stand-up men until it was time to stand-up. With the benefit of hindsight, these rats were no good from the beginning. They should never have been allowed into the mob. The men who backed them made the grave mistake of protecting them, supporting them, and allowing them into important leadership positions.

Sammy the Bull Gravano should have never been allowed to rise in position beyond soldier. Regardless of the money he brought into the Gambino Family, he should have never been made a captain let alone the underboss of the powerful crime family.

It was quite possible that the falling out Gravano had with his former friend Tommy Spero in the Colombo Family, where he had no representation, could have gotten him killed. Thanks to Louie Milito, though, Gravano escaped the Colombo Family and became a made man in the Gambino Family.

For Louie, this should have been a moment to consider the warning that it's your best friend that usually becomes your worst enemy. He should have left Gravano to make his own way to becoming a made man. They would have remained friends and still continued to earn together.

As I said before, Gambino boss Paul Castellano, paid a lot of attention to the construction business, and the bosses did not get involved with the day-to-day business so they put a panel together. On the panel were one or two members from each family who would settle beefs or problems with the various construction businesses. Paul appreciated Gravano's and Louie's ability to earn and their knowledge of the construction business, so he put them on the panel.

Gravano was not involved in Paul's murder. There was absolutely no reason for him to be involved or to want a coup. He was a content soldier loving his earnings, his many freedoms, and his direct communication with the boss. John Gotti and Frankie DeCicco certainly did not include Gravano in the plot. They had no reason to. Gotti and DeCicco planned and pulled off the coup together. They shared the top spot. They were actually partners, splitting everything 50/50.

After they took control of the family, DeCicco removed Toddo Aurello, who had helped Louie Milito and Gravano become made men, as a captain. DeCicco just didn't like Toddo. DeCicco would have put Louie as the new captain of that crew, but Louie was in prison on tax charges. Instead, he made Gravano captain. When Louie returned home, he accepted being under Gravano. Sammy was Louie's best friend, and Louie went along with it.

As the Gambino Family's new boss and underboss, Gotti and DeCicco would go to a social club in Brooklyn on 86th Street to meet every Sunday. Then they would get into DeCicco's car and drive to the Ravenite Social Club in Little Italy. It was a big mistake for a boss and his underboss to have such a set schedule, and especially to drive in the same vehicle as part of that routine. It would make assassinations easier.

So, shortly after Paul's assassination, DeCicco was blown up in his car outside of Jimmy Brown's club on a Sunday. John was supposed to be with Frankie, except on that Sunday John was sick in bed.

With DeCicco gone, John now had complete power and control over the Gambino Family. The first thing he should have done was made one of his guys in Queens his underboss. However, the first mistake, the biggest mistake of his life, was making Gravano his underboss.

A boss who rises to power through assassination should keep himself surrounded by trusted men, or at least men that are loyal to his faction of the family. Gravano was neither. He was a Paul Castellano loyalist and should have never been elevated to even captain, let alone underboss.

John was blinded by the amount of money Gravano was bringing in through construction. Maybe it didn't occur to him that he was going to continue to receive the same amount of money either way.

Or perhaps Gotti thought the family would be held together with a stronger bond if a man from the Castellano faction was in the number two spot. That way the other side of the family would realize that they were not going to be kept lower, and they would have actual representation in the family with one of their own in the number two spot.

Everyone expected Gravano, once made underboss, to elevate his best friend, Louie, as the captain of his crew. Louie was supposed to be the captain. Instead, Gravano passed over Louie and made Louis "Big Louie" Vallario, a recently inducted made member, the captain.

Louie Milito, being Gravano's best friend and partner, voiced his resentment. He felt, because of their long and close relationship, that he should answer directly to Gravano, not through a captain, especially someone who wasn't a long-term veteran. As a result, Louie Milito refused to show Big Louie respect.

Maybe it was Gravano's power trip or his incredible greed, but he went to John Gotti for permission to kill Louie Milito, the man who'd saved his life and who was the reason Gravano was a made man of the Gambino Family.

At that point, John should have realized that Gravano was asking to kill his best friend. He should have also figured out that Gravano, once Louie Milito was out of the way, would have a 100 percent interest in the businesses the two men owned, including construction and the million-plus dollars they both had on the street. Instead, John gave the ok for the hit because he was so blinded by the bags of money Gravano was bringing him.

On March 8, 1988, Louie Milito disappeared. Gravano took control of all of their businesses. He made Louie's wife and kids move to Florida by telling them they were in harm's way. Gravano took over the Milito's used car lot as well.

Gravano killed a number of people, mainly personal friends, and partners in various businesses, who truly had no business being killed. As John used to say, "You can't trust a man who doesn't drink or gamble." Gravano neither drank nor gambled.

John should have followed his own instincts, but he didn't. In the life, violence, murder especially, is a last resort to serious problems or for self-preservation, not just for greed or money. Most of the men who turn rat act like the toughest guys. They indiscriminately use violence at the drop of a hat. It's a bad sign when a made man always wants blood. He cannot be trusted and could turn out to be a rat.

Michael "Mikey Scars" DiLeonardo is one such mobster who displayed the characteristics of a tough guy who had the potential to become a rat. He became a member of the Gambino Family in the late 1980s. As a made man, he didn't keep a low profile, which is truly necessary in the life.

A made man is not supposed to use violence indiscriminately, especially if it does not pertain to business. Of course, violence is a necessary tool for the mob to enforce their rules, their way of life, and their livelihood.

However, if a man is too violent, there should be careful consideration in proposing him for membership. If a man of excessive violence, especially unnecessary violence, happens to be inducted into the ranks of the Mafia, he should not be put into positions of power. He should be kept at the level of soldier. He should know little about the family and the bosses.

Mikey Scars operated as a soldier through many of the John Gotti years. Once John went to prison and Gravano, after testifying against John, went into the witness protection program, Mikey became close with John Gotti Jr. John Jr. was helping run things for his father who was still running the family from prison.

Mikey and John Jr. began socializing in nightclubs together and it wasn't long before John Jr. took a liking to Mikey. He moved Mikey from the soldier he was and promoted him to the rank of captain in the construction area. They became the best of friends, and John Jr. enjoyed the lucrative earnings from construction under Mikey.

There were many instances in which Mikey was violent for reasons other than business. One such instance was a night out in Brooklyn in the early 1990s. I was there when Mikey showed up at Pastels, a nightclub run by the Genovese people. It was fairly early in the evening, before the crowds showed up to drink and dance. He was walking by the bar and quickly, with no provocation, took a glass and smashed an innocent kid in the face. The Genovese guys looked at each other and thought, "Is this guy crazy? How could a made guy come into another family's club and disrespect them so nonchalantly?" When Mikey approached the Genovese men, he said, "He'll never do that again."

"Do what?"

Mikey said, "He didn't move fast enough for me to pass."

Not only did he smash the young guy in the face with a glass, but he showed no respect for the family who owned the club. Made men are always supposed to show the utmost respect for other made members. There are rules to be followed so the life can continue and profits can be made.

But if a guy like Mikey Scars can attack an innocent man and hurt him enough to send him to the hospital within minutes of entering a club, then he's no good. Mikey also disrespected another family inside that family's club. Just one example among many to show Mikey was always predisposed to being a rat. They are born, not made.

Unfortunately, John Gotti Jr. made the same mistakes as his father. He should have never made Mikey a captain because of his unnecessary violence. He should have never allowed him to know so much about the family. When the handcuffs came and Mikey was arrested for murder, he folded and gave up his best friend, John Jr. He's now in the federal witness protection program.

Chapter Six

Never Tell Anyone You Killed Someone

Vincent "Jimmy" Rotondo from Brooklyn was a longtime member of the DeCavalcante Family who operated out of North Jersey in the 1980s. When he was made captain, he was allowed to induct a few guys, one of whom was his son, Anthony. That Anthony Rotondo became a made man was a big surprise to many made members because he was a college graduate, not a street guy.

Jimmy was affiliated with the International Longshoremen's Association that ran the waterfront in Brooklyn. He rose to be underboss, second in command under DeCavalcante boss, Johnnie Riggi. In 1988, Jimmy was found sitting in his car in front of his house with a bullet in the back of his head. Why he was killed was never clear. Riggi denied that he knew anything. But Riggi felt bad for Jimmy's son, Anthony, and elevated him to captain.

Regardless of whether or not Riggi had anything to do with Anthony's father's murder, he should never have made Anthony a captain. He should have left him as a soldier and placed him under one of his trusted captains.

Regardless of how the events took place, Anthony had to have hated everyone in the family because of the murder of his father. Not only was he made captain, but he was allowed to induct another man into the family to be under him because he had no crew. Usually when a man is made a captain, he takes over an existing crew.

So Anthony Rotondo had his good friend, Anthony Capo, inducted into the DeCavalcante Family. Anthony Capo was from the South Beach area of Staten Island. He was only twenty-one years old at the time of his induction. He was a low-level drug dealer and user who overindulged. Just that fact alone should have been enough to prevent him from being associated with made members let alone becoming one.

Every man who gets inducted into a family has some of the unwritten rules revealed to him. One such rule is to never use drugs and to not associate in any way with anyone dealing in drugs. Made men aren't supposed to lend money, take bets, or have any dealings or activities with drug dealers. The higher-ups never actually investigate the names put in for membership. They go solely on the word of the soldiers sponsoring them.

Another rule that was supposed to always be followed is that if a made member sponsors a guy who becomes a rat, the sponsor must be killed. Because this rule was hardly ever enforced, guys proposing friends took it lightly.

Capo, being a young kid, did not understand the responsibility or the true meaning of being a made member of a mob family. He was the proverbial wild kid. Using his soon-to-be status as a made man, he shook down all the drug dealers that were his friends as well as the guys he used drugs with. He surrounded himself with other wild kids. They frequented Staten Island nightclubs, always fought and wrecked places.

Other wiseguys were annoyed that this kid was a made member and that they had to give him respect and sit with him over issues. He would start fights in other family's clubs, and he couldn't just be taken care of or taught a lesson because he was a made member of a family. So, long-term wiseguys had to give this punk respect and sit with him to hear his side of the story. He was not well liked by many a made man.

In Capo's versions of the calamitous incidents that he created, he was never at fault. One such incident occurred when Joey Bilotti, brother to the late Tommy Bilotti, a made member of the Gambino Family, had to meet with Capo over a fight that took place in a friends club on Staten Island. Capo, as usual, claimed his innocence and that the melee that ensued in Bilotti's friend's club was the other guy's fault.

Bilotti, already knowing Capo's reputation and his rampant disrespect for others, was not buying his story. Bilotti wanted some sort of compensation, or at least an official apology to his friend. Capo, being young and foolish, began yelling. They both got loud, and the moment Capo went to push Bilotti he was met with a powerful knockout punch. As Capo lay on the floor, Joey Bilotti stepped on him and walked away.

Capo went back to the DeCavalcante Family with a different version of the incident. The DeCavalcantes sent some people to speak with some of the Gambino people because made men are not supposed to raise their hands to other made men, and especially not step on another guy with such disrespect after a sucker punch.

The Gambinos told them to leave it alone, it wasn't a sucker punch. Capo went after Bilotti. They warned the DeCavalcante people that if they pushed the issue the Gambinos were going to want Capo's head.

The DeCavalcante men knew the Gambinos were a much larger and more powerful family and had to back down. They knew if they didn't, Capo would have to be removed. They decided to let it go with an apology, and DeCavalcante men assured all parties that Capo would tone it down and behave as a respectful man of honor. As was stated earlier, the signs of a rat are evidenced by excessive violence and disrespect.

Shortly after Capo was supposed to have been subdued and kept to a lower, nonviolent profile, there was another incident in a club. This time, he was at a Genovese-run nightclub in the Bay Ridge section of Brooklyn. Around 3:30 a.m., after a long night of drinking and abusing cocaine, Capo picked a fight with a smaller kid at the bar. The kid put up his hands to defend himself as Capo took a glass in an attempt to smash it into his face.

Unfortunately for Capo, the glass broke in his hand and cut it up. With blood flowing from his hand, Capo's friends intervened and rushed him to the hospital. With his tough-guy pride a little beaten down after receiving several stitches, Capo was very unhappy. The next day, instead of leaving the situation alone and realizing the prior night's activities were alcohol and drug fueled, a now sober Capo decided to round up some friends and hunt for the smaller kid in Brooklyn.

The smaller kid discovered Capo was actually a made man and wasted no time in having his family contact the Gambinos about the incident. At that point the kid was unaware that Capo was looking for him. Capo did not want to just find the kid and beat him, he was determined to find him and kill him. Again, was blood necessary? When a made man always wants violence and blood, he will most likely become a rat.

Once the Gambinos discovered this, they sent word right away to the DeCavalcantes. They all had to meet with Capo again. They were annoyed, but they had to give some credibility to Capo as a made member. However, it was ordered that the kid be left alone, right or wrong. All previous indications of Capo being out of control and being too much of a liability went completely unnoticed by the DeCavalcantes.

As time went on, Anthony Rotondo, Capo's friend and captain, became increasingly fed up with all of Capo's antics and problems. Rotondo was also disappointed with Capo's excessive drug use. They began to not get along.

Rotondo met with the DeCavalcante Family's acting boss at the time, Vincent "Vinny Ocean" Palermo, to complain about Capo and gain some guidance on how to handle their problems with him.

Vinny, surprisingly, took Capo away from Rotondo and had him answer directly to him. At that point, Vinny, the acting boss, should have realized that Capo had too many issues and problems, especially with drugs, to be trusted.

Not only did Vinny have Capo answer directly to him, but he had him do all his running around, meeting with other families, and learning privileged Mafia knowledge.

Once again, this was a huge mistake on the part of a high-ranking made member, an acting boss who placed a person with all the signs of a rat into a position to know the secrets and inner workings of the higher-ranking members of his family and other families. Vinny should have recognized that Capo was out of control, violent, disrespectful, and addicted. He should have kept Capo out of any family business.

Even if Vinny wasn't aware of Capo's issues, which he was because of the numerous sit downs that had been held about Capo, Vinny's captain had come to him with the problems Capo was causing.

When a captain in a family brings certain things to a boss's attention, the boss should respect his captain. In this case, Rotondo's problems with Capo were in addition to what was common knowledge of Capo's bad behavior with other families. Vinny should have placed Capo on the shelf, out of the way.

Many made men are "placed on the shelf" or pushed out of the way for just one instance of disrespect. Capo showed disrespect several times. One such instance was in the early 1980s at a disco owned by a Genovese associate. Blossoms was on Midland Avenue in Staten Island. It was a club where many made members from all the families would gather to drink and socialize.

Two regulars were present that evening, Frankie DeCicco and Joe Watts. Sammy the Bull Gravano and Louie Milito had showed up to meet with them. Joe Watts is a well-respected and well-liked associate with the Gambino Family. He is German-Irish and could never become a made member because he is not Italian, but he answered directly to the boss, Paul Castellano.

After midnight, Jerry Chilli, a made member of the Bonanno Family, who was known for excessive drinking and the loudness that always accompanied his drinking, showed up drunk. Jerry had an issue with Joe Watts concerning conflicting street business. He wanted to speak with Joe in private.

Gravano, knowing Joe was not a made member and Jerry was, accompanied them to the table to talk. It is protocol for a made member to always be present for an associate if there is an issue or a beef with a made member from another family.

During their discussion, Jerry was very loud and boisterous. As he was arguing with Joe, he said, "Who the fuck are you? You're nobody." Jerry was referring to the fact that Joe was an associate, not a made member, and he did not have to show him the respect he would have to give a made member.

Noticing Gravano was about to interject, Jerry said to Gravano, "He's not a friend of ours." Again, meaning Joe was not a made member. Made members refer to other made members in a number of ways: "friend of ours," "wiseguy," "goodfella," "made man," "button man," "Stromberg," and an old favorite, "dunski."

Gravano said, "He may not be made, but he answers directly to Paul." With that said Jerry should have toned it down and continued with the discussion in a more respectful manner, regardless of the disagreement. However, Jerry replied, "I don't give a fuck who he answers to!"

Gravano, taken back and almost not believing what he'd just heard, brought Louie Milito to the table. He wanted to have another made man witness what was happening because of the severity of what was said, and the likely consequences that would have to follow. Absolutely no one, especially someone from another family, can or should, in any circumstance, ever disrespect a boss.

Gravano told Louie, "Jerry just insulted our boss, and he's out of control." When they returned to the table, Frankie DeCicco accompanied them. Jerry then actually repeated his statement of disrespect, not caring who Joe answered to. As the argument was escalating, it looked like punches were going to be thrown.

Carli DiPietro, a well-respected made member of the Genovese Family, walked in as the argument escalated. He was there to meet with DeCicco, but noticed the commotion and also that his longtime friend Jerry Chilli was in the middle of it and alone. Seeing Jerry outnumbered and drunk, Carli quickly went to the table and excused Jerry as he grabbed him by the arm and escorted him out of the club.

When Carli returned to make apologies for his friend, they informed him of what had happened. As soon as Carli heard what Jerry had said, his response was, with a surprised and then somber face, "Well, then you know what to do." Carli knew that there could be no apology at that level. What Jerry had said was a serious infraction of disrespect, drunk or sober. Therefore, the Gambino men had to take the matter directly to Paul Castellano.

In normal circumstances, the men would make their captains aware of a disrespectful verbal affront. However, DeCicco and Joe answered directly to Paul. Two days later, there was a meeting in the back room at Tommaso's Restaurant on 86th Street in Brooklyn. The attendees were Paul, Mr. O'Neil Dellacroce, and Joe N. Gallo, the top administration of the Gambinos. Stefano "Little Stevie Beef" Cannone, acting boss of the Bonnanos, and their consigliere, Anthony Spero, also were present. Louie and Gravano were present because they were the two men who heard the insult. The top guys from these families were gathered because in all likelihood Jerry Chilli would have to be killed.

However, the decision reached by the end of the meeting was for Jerry Chilli to be stripped of his made-man status. He was no longer permitted to associate, meet, or interact with other made members in any of the families.

Jerry is a stand-up guy, not excessively violent, but occasionally allows alcohol to get the better of him and influence his words. This was one instance of disrespect that almost cost him his life, but instead it caused his membership status to be placed on the shelf.

Capo, though, was not a stand-up guy. He was involved in numerous incidents and displayed an excess of disrespect. That alone should have prompted higher-ranking members in the DeCavalcante Family to take action against him. Further evidence of the need for immediate serious action was what Rotondo told Vinny Ocean about Capo's dangerous drug abuse.

However, Vinny made the most ridiculous mistake by bringing Capo closer and involving him more in the family, as opposed to stripping Capo's status and pushing him aside. Now we come to the Fred Weiss murder, which brought out the rats.

In 1989, Fred Weiss was a Staten Island businessman in sanitation and a Trade Waste Association delegate living in New Jersey. The union was actually run by the Gambino Family, so Weiss answered to Gravano. Someone told Gravano and John Gotti that Weiss was talking to the feds.

Gravano sent a hit team out to New Jersey to silence Weiss before any real damage could be done. His men returned without the mission accomplished, saying, "Jersey is too hard. We don't know the streets. It's gonna be too hard to get away from his house." John reached out to Vinny Ocean to take care of Weiss as a favor.

Vinny was excited to do this favor for John. The Five Families didn't consider the DeCavalcante Family a real family because, while the DeCavalcante boss, Johnnie Riggi, was in prison, the family operated more like a gang. They were not organized. Riggi was a real man. He kept that family together and operating smoothly while he was on the streets. The Genovese Family always had the smaller families coming to them for guidance: the Colombos, the Bonannas, and the DeCavalcantes.

When the feds were putting pressure on organized crime in the mid-1980s, Vincent "Chin" Gigante, then boss of the Genovese Family, closed the doors on those families. With no access to the Genovese Family, Riggi began going to the Gambino boss, Paul Castellano, and made an alliance. As a matter of fact, Paul and Tommy Bilotti met with Riggi at the Country Club Diner in Staten Island on an evening shortly before Paul went to Sparks Steak House in Midtown Manhattan where he was assassinated. After Paul was killed, the DeCavalcantes were under Gotti.

After Riggi was convicted for racketeering in 1989, he took fifteen years without blinking an eye. His control over the DeCavalcante Family was limited because of his incarceration and the restrictions imposed on him in prison. Riggi placed John "Johnnie Boy" D'Amato as acting boss. D'Amato began palling around with John Gotti.

Both D'Amato and Gotti loved to gamble and drink. The problem with this was that Gotti was the head of the second most powerful family, and he had an almost endless supply of money coming in. D'Amato did not.

D'Amato tried to keep up with Gotti, but he was getting himself into trouble. He gambled well beyond what he could afford. To make matters worse, he was taking money from his captains and not paying them back. He owed a sizeable fortune all around. He then began taking money from the DeCavalcante Family slush fund. The fund had been set up by Riggi for DeCavalcante members, to cover their legal fees and provide them start-up capital when they were released from incarceration.

With the blessings of everyone in the DeCavalcante Family, D'Amato was assassinated and Vinny Ocean took over as acting boss. After D'Amato's removal, the DeCavalcante Family fell out of favor with the other families, even the Gambinos.

So, when John Gotti reached out through Gravano to Vinny to kill Weiss, Vinny was beyond elated. He told his men, "We do this for John it'll put us back on the map."

Vinny, again not thinking or just lacking the intelligence to be a competent crime boss, gave the murder assignment to Rotondo and Capo. After several attempts and missed opportunities, the two men just couldn't get it done.

One afternoon, after complaining to each other, Rotondo and Capo went to the nearby home of DeCavalante soldier Jimmy Gallo (no relation to Gambino consigliere Joe N. Gallo). At that moment, Gallo was entertaining thirty people in his backyard with a barbeque. Rotondo explained to Gallo about the difficulties they were having in getting to Weiss. Rotondo wanted Gallo to take care of it, immediately.

Not wanting to refuse a captain in the family, Gallo excused himself from his guests at the barbeque. He went to Weiss's house in the middle of the day to check out the area and see how he could carry out the job, then went back to his barbeque.

A few days later, Gallo shot Weiss in the driveway. Later, when he walked into a social event with many of the DeCavalcante Family members present, they all applauded him and patted him on the back, telling him, "good job," "great job." Gallo, a true stand-up member of the Mafia, was actually quite perturbed at the accolades. He told me later, "These fuckin' morons went and told everyone about the murder."

In the life, murder is necessary on occasion. However, the man committing the murder wants, if at all possible, no one to know of his deed. If you kill someone, never tell anyone. It's smart advice.

John Gotti, though, didn't follow this wisdom, and his every-man-tested rule was another one of his major mistakes. When Gotti took over as boss of the Gambino Family, he made it a rule in his family that every man must be tested by having to kill or, at minimum, participate in a murder. Participation included driving the man who would do the actual killing and helping with dismemberment and/or the disposal of the victim.

Common sense dictates that the least amount of people who know about a murder, the better. A good boss never talks about any of the guys killed. An important rule is to never talk about murders to anyone. Never mention the names of anyone killed. And never mention the names of anyone who did the actual killing.

When Chin Gigante was boss of the Genovese Family, he had a small circle of men that he used for killings. The Genovese Family had a higher regard for human life than the other families. Sometimes, though, murder was necessary. If someone had to be removed, no one in the Genovese Family knew who did it, or why. It was never mentioned and never speculated about. Silence and secrecy have always been one of the Genovese's strengths.

For the Gambinos and DeCavalcantes, that, unfortunately, wasn't always the case, and many men went to prison because of informants. When Gravano went bad, he told the feds about the Weiss murder, giving up Vinny Ocean, Jimmy Gallo, Anthony Capo, and Anthony Rotondo. But Gravano did not give up his own men in the murder conspiracy.

Capo didn't even make it to the detention center before making a deal with the feds. Once Vinny discovered that Capo had turned, then he began to cooperate with the government. Now the feds had an acting boss and a soldier of the DeCavalcante Family cooperating. Then Rotondo turned informant.

Vinny's bargaining chip in his deal with the feds was to name the Gambino soldiers involved in the original Weiss murder conspiracy. He named Frankie "Fab" Fabiano, Eddie Garafola, and Big Louie. Those men were directly under Gravano at the time of the Weiss murder, the original hit team that couldn't figure out New Jersey. Vinny also named Mikey Scars DiLeonardo who, of course, turned rat.

The Weiss murder and conspiracy shed light on the differences between men of honor and rats. It illustrates that men who are excessively violent and always looking for blood do not stand up in the end. They were born rats. It also shows the qualities of the men who are honorable and do stand up.

I am neither condoning nor endorsing the men in the life or the murders that are sometimes necessary because of the life. They stood up and did not turn rat. They are born men. Nothing could change them.

Johnnie Riggi was finishing up his fifteen-year prison sentence at the age of eighty-one when he got slapped with another eleven years because of Capo, Rotondo, and Vinny. At eighty-seven, Riggi was released from a federal medical prison in 2012. James Gallo, fifty-eight, took twenty-five years for the Weiss conspiracy that he was ordered to do by Rotondo. Eddie Garafola, in his sixties, got thirty years, and Big Louie took fifteen years.

Those men understood that if you do the crime you do the time, and you do not destroy other lives and families by becoming a federal witness. Those who are born rats do the most destruction and evil while they are in the life, and then destroy more lives and families to protect themselves instead of doing the time for their crimes.

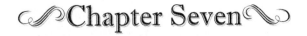Chapter Seven

LESSONS FROM THE COLOMBO WARS

I f your goal is power in a Mafia family, then you should plan this to the minutest detail, preparing for all possibilities well into the future. In the Mafia, as evident in the history of the Colombo Family, there is rampant betrayal and treachery. If you do not plan for every possibility, and most importantly, if you do not pay attention to the smallest details, then you won't achieve your goal. You will likely get assassinated.

In 1931, when Charles "Lucky" Luciano organized the Commission with the Five Families in New York City, Joe Profaci was the boss and founder of what later would be known as the Colombo Family, the last of the families to be organized. In the late 1950s, early '60s, Profaci used the Gallo crew, about forty to fifty men, to do a lot of work with very little earnings. Most of the work involved murders.

The main guys in this crew were Joseph "Crazy Joe" Gallo, Larry Gallo, and Carmine "Junior" Persico. They were desperate earners and wanted a bigger share or more compensation for the *work* they were doing. They were desperate because, unlike other Profaci Family members and higher-ups, they did not have rackets such as union shakedowns, capital to loan money on the streets for high interest, or gambling operations. They were forced to do robberies and heists. When they did work, such as hits for the boss, they were not cut in on any of the profits from the family's rackets.

The Gallo brothers became so dissatisfied with Profaci and the lack of financial interest, which they should have been getting, that on February 27, 1961 they and Carmine "Junior" Persico kidnapped Profaci's brother-in-law, Joseph Magliocco, Joe Colombo, a Profaci captain, and two other capos. They wanted the boss's attention, but that was not a well-thought-out plan.

Crazy Joe wanted to kill all of them and then go after Profaci to take over the family. Larry Gallo was more of a peacemaker, and he was trying to negotiate for a better share of the financial interests with their captives. Joe Colombo, a great speaker, convinced the Gallos to let them go and in return he would personally speak to the boss to work something out without any repercussions for the kidnapping.

In this violent world where murder is frequently used to resolve problems, the plans you make better be as flawless and as well thought out as possible. How could one truly believe that after kidnapping some of the top guys of a family there would not be serious repercussions? That is unless, of course, you do not fear or respect your opponents. To underestimate your opponent is another paramount mistake. You should treat every adversary with ruthlessness and respect.

The captives were released, but the Gallos got nothing. Colombo even convinced Junior Persico to switch sides. Larry Gallo never suspected the betrayal. He was sent for to discuss a deal at the Sahara Lounge, a supper club in Brooklyn. The deal that awaited him was death.

On August 20, 1961, like a scene out of *The Godfather, Part II*, which is probably where the moviemaker got the idea, Larry Gallo was being strangled when a cop walked into the bar. The cop's partner was shot, but the strangulation wasn't completed. The Gallos went to war. This was the first Colombo war.

Things soon quieted down for a while because of several events: Crazy Joe Gallo was arrested on extortion charges and sent away for fourteen years in a New York State penitentiary; Joe Profaci developed terminal cancer and died about a year later in 1962, making Magliocco the boss; and a couple of Gallo guys went to jail. Larry Gallo developed cancer and would die in his sleep in 1968.

Junior Persico and his brother, Alphonse "Allie Boy" Persico, always had a burning desire for power. They made up their minds before being inducted into the Mafia in the early 1950s that they were not just going to be soldiers, but bosses. Their goal from the beginning was to take power.

The Persicos followed strict guidelines and rules as tough guys of the street. They were willing to act quickly and violently, but most importantly, they planned the details and stayed patient, all of which is necessary for getting power successfully.

When they were in their early twenties—this was in the early '50s—there was an older guy in their neighborhood who called a lot of the shots. His name was Stevie Bovi. Although they were close to Bovi, they wanted him out of the way so that they could call their own shots.

One night, Bovi climbed into a car with Allie Boy and Junior. Bovi sat in the front seat and one of the Persicos shot him to death from the backseat. The police caught the driver of the car, a guy named Blue Beetle, and Allie Boy. Beetle cooperated with the government and Allie Boy was convicted of the murder. He was sentenced to twenty years in prison. However, as many know, Junior Persico was the actual murderer.

After the trial, Beetle was walking along 5th Avenue near 3rd Street when a few of Persico's friends, gang members, grabbed him and wrestled him to the ground. They shoved his head under a car and were about to run it over when men ran out of a DeCavalcante Family social club and stopped them. A fight ensued. Beetle escaped.

At that time, it was a close-knit Italian neighborhood and most men were very respectful toward another's family. Beetle's mother begged the Persicos for her son's life. Respectful of the mother, they decided to spare Beetle's life, but on the condition that Beetle had to leave New York forever.

About five years later, Beetle returned from California to visit his mother for Christmas. During his visit he began to feel comfortable and stayed much longer after the holiday was over. He became so comfortable he began playing cards in a DeCavalcante social club. One night, while he was playing cards, two men with ski masks entered the club. While one of the guys held everyone at bay saying, "We are not robbing you," the other guy fired his weapon into Beetle's head, killing him.

The Persicos showed they were men to be feared and respected. They showed qualities of compassion, as well as extreme ruthlessness, if crossed. They displayed the toughness, the street smarts, the respect, and the earmarks of men, not only with a thirst for power, but the qualities that would make great Mafia bosses.

Junior Persico was known as "the Snake" for his betrayal of the Gallo brothers, but his ambitions for power were meticulously calculated. After the kidnapping, he knew the Gallo brothers lacked what it took to be real leaders. He knew his ambitions would be cut down early if he stayed with the Gallos. He had the wisdom to switch sides, which kept him moving toward his goal of ultimate power.

When Joe Profaci died in 1962, his brother-in-law, Tony Magliocco, took over the Profaci Family. Joe Bonanno, boss of the Bonanno Family, devised a plan to remove the other bosses of the Commission, with Magliocco's help. Magliocco joined Bonanno because the Commission perceived him as weak and were not inclined to recognize him as the official boss of the Profaci Family.

Magliocco's part in this conspiracy was to have Carlo Gambino, boss of the Gambino Family, and Tommy Lucchese, boss of the Lucchese Family, killed. Once they removed the bosses of those two families, they would make a captain from each family that owed loyalty and allegiance to Magliocco and Bonanno a boss.

Of course, if your goal is to gain more power and wealth, this would be a critical part of the plan. However, a plan such as taking out the bosses of other families should be devised in such a manner as to account for all variables. And before that plan is discussed with anyone, it should be finalized with the fewest and most trusted of your men.

During the planning of this conspiracy, it was agreed to send Joe Colombo to kill Carlo Gambino because they were friends. Colombo, a captain, was trusted and well-liked by Carlo, so they figured Colombo was their best chance to get close enough to kill Gambino.

It may be necessary at this point to clarify one of the rules concerning killing in the Mafia. An associate begins by earning money and proving himself to be valuable to the made man he is accountable to. If he is seen as truly valuable, the made man he is under will ask, "What are your intentions?"

The meaning of this question presented to the associate is whether he intends to become a made member or not. If he wants to become a member of the Mafia the next question is, "Are you willing to kill someone?" If the answer is no, depending on his earning abilities, he is most likely let go and never bothered with again. If he says yes, he accepts the responsibility and is informed that he could be called on at any time to kill someone while he is an associate or at any point after being made.

Of course, if he is called upon to kill as an associate and refuses, he is let go and cut off or he is killed. If the time to kill comes while he is a soldier and he doesn't do it, he is killed. You either kill, as per the request from the boss and/or higher-ups, or you are killed, simple as that.

One misconception is that every member of the Mafia had to personally kill to be inducted. As an associate, just saying you are willing to kill, especially if you are a good earner, is enough for you to be inducted. However, it is quite possible for someone to go through his entire life as a made member never having to kill anyone.

Joe Colombo was a good earner, but he wasn't a tough guy, not muscle. He was adept at negotiating and verbal communications. He was known to have "a golden tongue." Whether he ever killed anyone is unknown. His goals were more for money and wealth than for ultimate power. Of course, being the boss of a family will bring you plenty of both.

Colombo made a wise move instead of following through with his boss's plans. The Gambino Family was a much bigger and stronger family than the Profaci Family. If he'd murdered Carlo Gambino, Magliocco would have gained more power, wealth, and influence. Colombo's fate would have been much more uncertain, even if he was promised more of a share in the family's profits. It was wiser to side up with his friend who was the boss of a much stronger family because the benefits would far outweigh the alternative.

Colombo betrayed his boss and informed Gambino of the plot, and gained much more for himself. When it got out that Gambino knew of the intended plot, Magliocco, already ill, died of a heart attack and Joe Bonanno fled to Arizona.

Gambino met with the Genovese Family for Joe Colombo. The Genovese had a lot of influence in the dealings and arrangements of all of the families. Both families agreed to anoint Joe the new boss of the Profaci Family, which later became known as the Colombo Family.

Joe Colombo's betrayal of his boss secured his future and gave him power and complete reign over the family. Colombo had the full backing of Gambino and was in the good graces of the Genovese Family.

At this point, the Colombo Family was a small but close-knit family. There were four main captains overseeing the crews: Charlie "Moose" Panarella in Staten Island; Dominick "Mimi" Scalo, with the biggest crew of about forty guys, in Coney Island, Brooklyn; Greg Scarpa Sr. on 13th Avenue in Brooklyn; and Junior Persico in South Brooklyn. Businesses and the life were running smoothly for Colombo as boss and for his family.

In 1971, Crazy Joe Gallo was released from prison after serving ten years. He returned to New York City and so did the old beefs. Gallo was more than just displeased that, in his mind, a weak man was now the boss. Gallo did not approve of or respect Joe Colombo as boss of the family. This was the same guy who'd been trapped in a warehouse and talked his way out of being kidnapped by falsely promising Gallo and his men a better deal.

Also, Colombo's captain was Junior Persico, who had betrayed the Gallos after the kidnapping incident. Joe Gallo was not pleased that after ten years his crew was still not treated as he felt they should be. He still wanted his better deal.

Colombo sent two captains, Rocky Miraglia and Nicky Bianco, to the Gallo stronghold on President Street, between Columbia and Van Brunt streets, in South Brooklyn. They brought Gallo $20,000 as a welcome home present. Joe Gallo threw the money back at them yelling, "I'll deal with that scumbag myself!" Then he chased them off the block.

While Joe Gallo was away, his younger brother Albert Gallo became close with Vincent "Chin" Gigante, then a captain in the powerful Genovese Family. It was a way for the Gallo crew to build, but Joe Gallo wanted his own thing. Albert had also recruited a bunch of younger guys in his brother's absence. Those guys all looked up to Joe because of his reputation and felt that once Joe came home things would get better.

The guys Albert recruited included Bobby and Stevie Boriello, Stevie Cirillo, and Preston Geritano. Joe took those guys and raised havoc against Joe Colombo and attempted a few assassinations against Junior Persico. He would go into clubs and other businesses owned by or affiliated with Joe Colombo and claim them as his own. He took over illegal enterprises he felt should have been his during his ten-year absence.

Furthermore, once he came home, he sent word to the older guys that had been a part of his crew, telling them that they belonged to him. Many of his former guys had formed alliances with Colombo men in his absence. Some were doing business on their own.

John "Mooney" Cutrone, the only made guy besides Joe Gallo, operated out of a luncheonette on Avenue M that he owned. Smoky and Johnny "Tarzan" Lusterino ran a bookmaking operation out of their car service on 10th Avenue and 39th Street. Jerry Basciano and Frank "Punchy" Illiano hung out on 86th Street with Colombo guys. Sammy the Syrian and Louie the Syrian were still with Al Gallo on President Street.

Joe Gallo's message to his old crew was, "Come back where you belong or go get a lunch pale and go to work because you're through in this life." A lot of the guys went back with much bitterness. They felt they were better off with half a loaf than with no loaf. They knew that in going back to Gallo there was going to be a lot of trouble and less earning. Once again, Gallo was making moves for power without having clear-cut and well-thought-out plans. He was operating on his reputation and the fear that many men had of him.

He acted in accordance with his nickname, Crazy Joe. He would pull up across the street from the Diplomat Lounge on 3rd Avenue and Carol Street, a Persico stronghold, making sure he was seen. He would grab guys on the street he knew were around the Persicos and give his regards, knowing they were all reaching for their guns.

Another rumor that earned him his moniker was an incident that occurred when Joe Colombo was coming out of Scarpaci's Funeral Home on 86th Street. Allegedly, Crazy Joe pulled up in a car filled with his guys. He got out, and a shoving match started between Colombo's guys and Gallo's guys. Crazy Joe grabbed Colombo and shook him saying, "The next time I see you it will be the last." Now, Crazy Joe was definitely crazy. After an arrest in 1950, Gallo was placed in Kings County Hospital in Brooklyn where he was diagnosed with schizophrenia.

But Joe was also crazy for another reason. If you are going to make a power move against a boss of a family, plans should be well thought out with clear goals and details along with the proper alliances and backings. Not under any circumstances do you do the things Crazy Joe was doing, because the only goal you will achieve is your death and the ruination of the lives of everyone around you.

If Gallo was making a play to take the family, he should have at least killed Colombo instead of shaking him. The only plan that Joe seemed to have was to be a thorn in everyone's side. Colombo, perhaps thinking he could appease Gallo on his release from prison and possibly make him an ally, had offered him $20,000.

Colombo, though, should never have forgotten Gallo's reputation and should've known that Crazy Joe would demand a lot more than a $20,000 insult. Perhaps Colombo should have made him a captain and straightened out some of his men by inducting them into the Mafia.

But Colombo seemed not to care about the Gallos or their men. In this case, a boss with a clear goal of maintaining his power and position should have eliminated Crazy Joe the moment he was released from prison or at least while he was doing time.

Knowing Gallo was a problem and crazy should have convinced Colombo that he needed a few clear alternate plans for killing Gallo. Colombo's misstep was costly to him on many levels, mostly to his reputation as boss. He lost the respect of his men and the respect of other families.

As I stated earlier, Joe Colombo's focus was more on money and wealth rather than ultimate power. He was handed the position of boss by the Commission as a result of his betrayal of Magliocco and as a reward from Gambino. He did not take the top spot, and that was something that many in his family, especially Crazy Joe, did not respect.

Colombo had ruled during peace and wasn't tested until Crazy Joe's release. It was a test he failed. Prior to Gallo's release from prison, no one in the family, even if they thought about it, would ever have made a move to take over.

Regardless of Colombo not being a tough guy or not having a clear and strong plan to maintain power, he always had the backing of the Gambino Family and the Genovese Family. Real men of ambition with clear plans for power would never make a move that would incite other families to strike. The biggest rule is, "You never kill a boss."

Junior Persico enjoyed his position as captain in the family and the money he earned. While Gallo was away it was peaceful and businesses ran smoothly. During this time, Persico continued to increase his power, his capital reserves, and his influence. He planned for the day when the opportunity would arise for him to take power.

Colombo had an eight-year run as the boss while the federal government kept at him. The government's relentless pursuit of Colombo and his sons prompted him to form the Italian American League. The league claimed that Italian Americans were treated poorly, unfairly, and discriminated against by the government. The league picketed the FBI building in Manhattan. In 1970, Colombo held a rally in Columbus Circle in which more than 100,000 Italian Americans showed up to support. He had businesses, anything mob-owned and/or Italian-owned, shut down for the day.

It was a mistake for Colombo to show law enforcement the strength and influence of the league. It may have been a legitimate gripe of many Italian Americans who felt they were treated unfairly and often stereotyped, but the man who founded and operated the league was in fact an actual boss of a Mafia family.

As I stated earlier, if your ambition is to be a boss of a crime family, you must plan well into the future to attain and secure power. If you are not willing to do so, you should never think of entering the life to begin with.

One of the Mafia's strengths is supposed to be its secrecy. If you manage to attain the position of boss, you should keep as low a profile as possible in the outside world, especially in regard to law enforcement and the government. In order to continue to make profits from illegal enterprises, you want no attention whatsoever. Colombo was bringing unnecessary attention to himself and the rest of the families.

The Genovese and Gambino families, the largest and most powerful families, told Colombo to step down from the league and put a legitimate guy up front. Colombo felt he was a great speaker—and he was, but he was also a mob boss—and the league needed him to be involved all of the time. He did not listen to their warnings.

The following year, 1971, Colombo had his guys and the league telling Italian businesses to shut down again for the next rally. The Genovese and Gambino families told everyone to stay open. At the rally, Colombo was gunned down by Jerome Johnson, an African-American hustler who authorities believe the Gambino's hired to kill Colombo. A second assailant in the crowd shot Johnson to death and fled. Colombo survived from getting shot in the head and neck, but he suffered severe brain damage and remained paralyzed until his death seven years later.

Colombo was taken out because he violated some cardinal rules in the Mafia: he did not have clear plans; he did not act decisively and quickly; he brought attention to himself and his family; and he allowed his reputation to be tarnished.

In the life, your reputation, if nothing else, is the most important and valuable thing you have. Any sign of disrespect or trouble from a subordinate should be dealt with swiftly. Colombo allowed Crazy Joe Gallo's antics to minimize the respect of his own men and other families. When your men no longer respect you, your authority, your leadership, or your power, the consequences can be terminal.

Chapter Eight

Persicos Rise to Power

After Joe Colombo was shot, leadership in the family was up for grabs because there was still no plan for the continuation of a ruling structure. The underboss had become too old. With no clear line of succession for the ruling regime, powerful captains were free, in a sense, to make moves to secure the top seats and grab power.

Junior Persico grabbed the opportunity and took control of the Colombo Family; but Persico was headed to prison on contempt charges. His brother Allie Boy and Dominick "Mimi" Scialo were meeting often to plan, map out, and consolidate power in order to take over the family with Junior as the boss.

In one such meeting in 1974, Scialo was drinking in excess. He was known to be a drinker who often allowed alcohol to get the better of him. Scialo, in the past, had hurt a lot of people for no reason because of his drinking. At this meeting, as they discussed the family's proposed structure, positions, and operations, Scialo purposely would not mention Junior's name. Allie Boy had to keep interjecting that Junior was going to be the real boss of the family. Finally, after more drinks, Scialo said, "Fuck Junior. What do we need him for? We can do this without him."

I will point out that although it is socially acceptable and perhaps routine for guys in the life to drink and even drink in excess, it should be unacceptable for a boss or a made man to become inebriated. A boss, and even a made man, should, in fact, for countless reasons, not drink alcohol at all.

Here's one example why. With that simple, "Fuck Junior," comment, Scialo sealed his fate. Regardless of Scialo's drunkenness and his reputation for letting alcohol screw him up, in the Mafia, where the stakes are high for money and power, you cannot afford to take little chances or overlook slights.

At the next meeting, things were going smoothly and Scialo was sober. Then, a made man known as Scappie proceeded to stab Scialo ten times, ending his life and any possibility of future harm to the Persicos' power. They carried him through the back of Monte's Restaurant, through the yards, and buried him in the basement of a social club on President Street.

Tony Ricciardi and Tommy Barbusca were two of Scialo's top guys. They were loyal to Scialo, very tough, and they knew about Scialo and the Persicos' plans to take over the family. When Scialo disappeared, they suspected something had happened and demanded the whereabouts of their captain. They should have realized that for whatever reason something went wrong and that the Persicos were taking control without Scialo. They should have never voiced their concerns so loudly during a regime change.

If they were going to do anything about what had happened, they should have quietly bided their time and made alliances and allegiances with the right men to seek revenge in the future. But one night shortly after the disappearance of Scialo, Tony and Tommy were drinking in the club in Brooklyn. At the end of the night when they both got into the car, an assassin fired a shotgun through the windshield and killed them both. Regardless of whether their complaints had anything to do with their murders, they were dangerous men. Their captain disappeared after a meeting with Allie Boy. The Persicos acted swiftly and removed a potential problem, if not an immediate problem.

As the Persicos stepped in to take control of the Colombo Family, they did everything necessary and acted in a manner that men in positions of power are supposed to act. They knew there was no room for error. They knew they could not overlook anything, even a thorn.

Joe Gallo was a thorn in Colombo's side. And he was still around during the regime change. One night, while Crazy Joe was in the Copacabana in Manhattan with a few of his young Turks, he spotted Russ Buffalino, the boss of Northeast Pennsylvania's Buffalino crime family. Knowing Buffalino was close to the Persicos, Crazy Joe went out of his way to verbally abuse him; a paramount mistake if one values his life.

Once the Persicos heard, they put out an open contract on Joe Gallo. He was to be shot on sight. About a month later, on April 7, 1972, Gallo celebrated his birthday at the Copacabana with his wife, daughter, sister, and two bodyguards. One of his bodyguards, Bobby Darrow, met a woman, who wanted to go home with him. Bobby did not want to leave Gallo. However, as I was told, Gallo, joking around, embarrassed Bobby into leaving with the woman. "What are you, a faggot? You gotta go."

After seeing the show and having a few drinks, Gallo and his family headed to Umberto's Clam House on the corner of Mulberry and Hester streets in Little Italy to have a late bite to eat. While walking into the restaurant, a Colombo associate spotted him and made some phone calls. A short while later, Joe Yacovelli, the Colombo Family's consigliere, and his men entered and gunned down Gallo, killing him.

95

It was well known that Gallo did a lot of reading while incarcerated. When he was released from prison he often quoted *The Prince* by Machiavelli, the Italian Renaissance philosopher and writer. Many of his men were uneducated and probably never read a book. They were all very impressed and followed Gallo because they perceived him as strong, tough, and educated.

It must be clarified that although Gallo read a lot and was able to quote many passages, he didn't understand what he read. He didn't act according to what he read. The equivalent is the religious zealot who continuously quotes scripture and passages from the Bible, but has no clue what it means and does not act according to what he is quoting.

If Gallo had truly learned from what he'd read, he would not have acted the way he did. He would have prudently planned for a true power play, took his time, built his capital reserve, made proper alliances, and anything else that would ensure not only his ambitions for power, but his existence.

Once Joe Gallo was laid to rest, the Gallo crew, understandably upset, began to fire shots. The second Colombo war had begun.

The Gallos got a tip that Yacovelli, Gennaro "Gerry Lang" Langella, Allie Boy Persico, and another Colombo guy were meeting in the Neapolitan Noodle, a restaurant on Manhattan's East 79th Street. One of the Gallos dressed as a woman, but didn't know what either Langella or Persico looked like. He went in and shot the wrong men who were sitting at the bar, killing two and wounding two others. Meanwhile, Persico, Langella, Yacovelli and the other guy were in their seats in the dining room.

Once those two innocent civilians were murdered, the other families got involved. Joe Brancato, a captain in the Colombo Family, was favored by Carlo Gambino because he was an old-timer. In 1973, Brancato became acting boss, Allie Boy was made acting consigliere to make the Persicos happy, and Yaccovelli became acting underboss. To keep the peace, the Gallo crew answered to Brancato, who promised to do right by them.

While his brother Junior was away in prison, Allie Boy feared that if Brancato did a good job the other bosses would recognize him as the official boss. If that occurred, the Persicos, who did a lot of work to grab power, would be back where they started.

Junior did not like the decision to name Brancato acting boss. He believed the Persicos' plans and ambitions for the top spot were in jeopardy. Junior, knowing the Genovese Family had most of the say with everything, directed Allie Boy to go to Alphonse "Funzi" Tieri, the street boss of the

Genovese Family. Brancato was only acting boss for a few months before going to prison for murder and Tom DiBella became acting boss of the Colombo Family.

Meanwhile, the other bosses recognized Junior as the official boss. The other bosses felt he was the rightful boss of the Colombo Family because he did all of the work and he was more likely to keep a stronghold over his men.

Once Junior was recognized, the Persicos immediately put together their ruling administration. DiBella became the figurehead boss, meaning the family would be run by Junior, but DiBella would front as the boss. This was a wise move to keep the spotlight off of Junior and make it easier for Junior to hold on to power. Allie Boy became the official consigliere. Langella became the official underboss.

The Persicos, to ensure their power, broke down many of the captains to soldiers and put Persico men in their place. Brancato, previously the acting boss, was broken down to soldier and placed under a loyal Persico captain. This move, once again, placed the Gallos in limbo. They did not get any of their men straightened out, and they lost any recognition they had with Brancato. The Gallos were the mortal enemies of the Persicos.

When those moves were made in 1974, dissension among the Gallos grew. The older guys—Jerry Basciano, John "Mooney" Cutrone, Sammy the Syrian, Smoky, and Johnny "Tarzan" Lusterino—left the Gallo stronghold on President Street. Frank "Punchy" Illiano, Louie the Syrian, and the younger guys stayed with Al Gallo.

As you've surely noticed, the distinguishing characteristic of a mobster is the nickname, a trait mostly among Italian mobsters. It came out of the New York neighborhoods, usually derived from a man's appearance, behavior, skill, business, or job.

Most of us made men only knew one another by our nicknames or first names, and our first names often weren't actually our real names. Rarely would we know each other's real name until a guy was arrested and his actual full name, along with his nickname, was reported in the newspapers. For example, I never knew that Sammy Meatballs' last name was Aparo until I read it in the paper.

As more and more guys were being arrested and convicted in the 1990s, some of the bosses realized nicknames were making them federal targets. Nicknames recorded from wiretaps and bugging, along with the help of informants, made it easier for the feds to identify a Mafia member when a nickname was dropped in conversation. So, they tried to start a policy of not using nicknames. I don't think it worked.

In July 1974, to save face, some of the younger guys who stayed with Gallo were sent out to shoot Basciano. He was going into the Cobble Hill Car Service on Sacket and Court streets when they fired from outside into the car service. Basciano was wounded in the shoulder. At the same time, a crew was sent out after Mooney, but he spotted the shooters, jumped over a car, and ran away. Smoky tried to run into a car service, tripped and fell. The shooters, not wanting to kill him, just shot him in the leg.

At this point, Basciano and Mooney Cutrone were joining the Persicos, which was a big mistake because there has always been bad blood there. The Persicos used it as an opportunity to have both factions wipe each other out; in essence, they were doing the work that the Persicos were going to do anyway. When you are in a position of power like the Persicos, it is wise to use others to do your dirty work, especially when you stand to gain even more from the results, like having your enemies kill each other off.

In August 1974, Gallo loyalist Stevie Cirillo and some of the younger guys were at a Vegas Night event when a bullet was fired, killing Stevie. "Funzi" Tieri, street boss of the Genovese Family, sat down with Allie Boy and DiBella and told them, "As of right now, the Gallos belong to us."

That fall, with the relationship that Al Gallo now had with Chin Gigante, the Genovese Family tells the Persicos, "All of this violence has to stop, or we will handle it." In the Mafia, this was unheard of without it being amicably discussed and agreed upon, and it was especially unheard of for a family to take an entire crew of more than ten men. Now, anyone in the Gallo crew was untouchable. The Persicos had to leave them alone.

The Persicos, of course, did not like that the Gallos were now untouchable, but they had their troubles with the other faction of that crew permanently eliminated. Still, the war continued. In 1976, with the Persicos sanctioning the older guys to retaliate, Basciano hired a sniper. The sniper settled into an abandoned building with a clear shot of the corner of President and Colombia streets, the Gallo stronghold.

The first Gallo casualty was Louie the Syrian, who was standing on the corner talking to a couple of guys when he was shot in the back. He was confined to a wheelchair for the rest of his life. The second Gallo casualty was Stevie Boriello, who was shot in the face as he walked down the block.

A few months later, a meeting was arranged for Jerry Basciano to meet with a Genovese captain at Frank's Diner on Union and Nevins streets. As the two men were sitting and talking, a gunman wearing a ski mask walked into the diner and blew Basciano's head off, splattering it against the wall. Mooney Cutrone, who frequented a neighborhood coffee shop on Avenue N every morning, was killed by a gunman wearing a ski mask. After coming out of his house one morning, Sam "Sammy the Syrian" Zahralbam was chased down the block by a gunman wearing a ski mask. He was hit in the leg. There were too many witnesses around, so the gunman was unable to finish the job. Sammy recovered from his wounds and moved to California. He was never heard from again.

Later that year, the Persico's father passed away. At the wake, held in Scarpaci's Funeral Home on 86th Street, many powerful Mafia figures were in attendance. Funzi, the Genovese Family street boss, also attended, accompanied by Al Gallo. He made it a point to introduce Al Gallo to the top Persico guys as his "son."

Chin Gigante had Funzi do this to send a clear message to the Persicos that if anything were to happen to Al Gallo the consequences would be worse than hell.

CℛChapter Nineℛ

Persicos Fall — Gotti Rises

While things were running smoothly for the Persicos, Junior came home from prison in 1979. It was the first time the two brothers, Junior and Allie Boy, were home together in a long time, but their reunion was short lived.

In 1980, Allie Boy got indicted on extortion charges. He'd loaned the son of Anthony Cantalupo, a real estate businessman, $10,000. The son, Joseph, fell behind on the vig and began to avoid the Persicos. One day in the Diplomat Bar, a Persico stronghold on 3rd Avenue, Allie Boy and one of his soldiers, Mike Ballino, beat the son up pretty good with kicks and punches, and then demanded that he start paying and stop hiding.

After that incident, the son wore a wire. Ballino was arrested and Allie Boy fled, to be apprehended seven years later. He hadn't served more than two years of his twenty-five-year sentence when he died at sixty-one of cancer of the larynx.

While Allie Boy was on the lam, it was business as usual with Junior, the official boss of the family, running things the way they should be run. He enjoyed approximately five years of ruling the family outside of prison before the Commission case arose. As stated earlier, the Commission of the American Mafia consists of the bosses and/or their representatives. At certain points in time, they would meet to rule on interfamily disputes, profits, and more. Its main function was to settle underworld problems.

In early 1985, after audio and video surveillance combined with informants, the federal government arrested whoever happened to be present at any of the Commission meetings being held during their extensive surveillance. This became known as the Commission case. Genovese boss, Fat Tony Salerno; Gambino boss, Paul Castellano; the whole Lucchese administration, including Tony Ducks Corallo the boss, Tom Mix Santoro the underboss, and Christie Tick Furnari the consigliere; and Colombo boss, Junior Persico and underboss, Gerry Langella. The Bonannos were not sitting on the Commission at that point in time.

After Junior was arrested in February 1985, he never returned home. In 1986, he was sentenced to a hundred years in prison. Everyone was arrested with no bail, including Langella and Scappie. At the same time, Tom DiBella, the figurehead boss, became bedridden with cancer. While Junior was in the Manhattan Correctional Center (MCC) fighting the Commission case, Joseph "Joe T" Tomasello from Avenue U became acting boss, and Vincent "Jimmy" Angelino became acting consigliere for the Colombo Family.

Within a couple of years of holding this position, Jimmy Angelino conspired to take over the family. He felt, with most of the top guys going to prison, the family was weak enough for him to carry out his plans. It is unknown who he was conspiring with, but that person gave him up immediately.

One of the Persicos' strengths was the loyalty and respect of their soldiers. Not all members of the Colombo Family were Persico loyalists, but those that were knew their place. Jimmy Angelino was, in fact, an original Persico guy, and most likely the person he trusted was one as well.

Another trait that helped the Persicos rise to power, and to hold on to that power, was their ability to move swiftly and fiercely. In 1988, Jimmy Angelino disappeared. Carmine Sessa, the consigliere, confessed to the murder after becoming a government witness. He is reportedly still in the federal witness protection program.

All the defendants in the Commission trial, including Junior, were convicted. Once Junior knew he wasn't coming home, he put up an acting administration that consisted of Vic Orena as the acting boss, Benny Aloi as acting consigliere, and Wild Bill Cutolo as the acting underboss. They were to run the day-to-day operations and keep the family together and functioning smoothly. Their other function was to collect the money owed to the official administration and pass it on.

In 1991, Benny Aloi went to jail on an extortion and conspiracy conviction for his role in the Windows case, fixing the bid process on thermal windows for public housing projects. Benny died in 2011. Benny's incarceration left Wild Bill and Vic Orena to run the Colombo Family alone. It ran well—for a while.

When John Gotti took over the Gambino Family in 1985, his ego got in the way, and he made many mistakes. He had a true hunger and thirst to be the boss of bosses, but he had to contend with the Genovese and Lucchese families. He wrapped up the smaller families under him. New Jersey's DeCalvacante Family and the Bonanno Family in New York owed him allegiance, especially when the Genovese closed the doors to those families.

After the feds sent Junior to Lompoc Federal Correctional Complex in California, Colombo acting boss, Vic Orena, began to buddy up to John, giving John the opportunity to wrap up another family. But Vic constantly complained to confidants that he and Wild Bill were "just money collectors."

Vic and Wild Bill had all of the responsibilities and risks of being the ruling administration with none of the benefits, including the money. As anyone who is incarcerated knows, it is very difficult to hold on to the business from prison.

The Persicos did well to keep themselves in power and always have loyalists on the street. Maybe they should have offered or allowed Vic and Wild Bill to pocket some of the money they were collecting for the family's administration, especially since they were never coming home.

If they had made that offer, though, it may have been perceived as a sign of weakness. Vic and Wild Bill were not the happiest acting bosses, but when the boss of the second most powerful crime family added fuel to the embers, things happened.

During the Commission case trial, Junior decided to defend himself. He thought he would be able to cross-examine witnesses in a way a defense lawyer could not. Gotti frowned upon it. His opinion was that a boss of a family should never defend himself in court. Wild Bill had a connection with the feds and was able to get the minutes of the trial, specifically, the minutes of Junior's defense, to Gotti.

Gotti told Vic Orena that he would bring the transcript to the Commission. At that time, the Commission bosses consisted of John Gotti, Chin Gigante, and Vic Amuso of the Lucchese Family.

Gotti went back to Vic Orena and told him that the Commission voted to take Junior down. He named Vic the new boss of the Colombo Family with the backing of the Gambino Family. With this, Vic pulled in all the men of the family and told them the news. Eleven Persico loyalists, captains, and wiseguys refused to go along.

When word reached Junior in prison, he sent two of his captains to meet with the Genovese Family to find out whether what Gotti said was true. The Genovese guys denied there was any such Commission meeting. However, they also said, "We are neutral. We will recognize any administration you guys put together."

Gotti wrote the eleven names of the Persico loyalists on paper and gave it to his captains to show the Gambino soldiers. Those men were not to be recognized by any Gambinos, they were now outlaws. The first thing was for Vic and Wild Bill to lock up all of the money. They now had the full backing of John and the entire Gambino Family.

Unfortunately for Vic, shortly after that move Gotti, Gravano, and Gambino consigliere, Frank "Frankie Loc" LoCascio are arrested without bail. Meanwhile, the Commission, worried about another war, refused to recognize Vic as the Colombo boss.

As I said, John had a huge ego. He thought he was untouchable because the media called him the "Teflon Don," but he should have put into place a number of backup plans in case he was incarcerated. He was making serious power moves to become the dominant force in the Mafia. It was more of a pipe dream, but nonetheless, he was making power moves. He should have had a contingency plan for a number of men to continue to back Vic and his play for power.

Because Gotti didn't have a contingency plan when he was arrested, the Gambino Family left the Colombo Family to have another factional fight. This was 1990 and the start of the third Colombo war. The eleven Persico loyalists went after Vic, Wild Bill, and their men while Vic sent his men after them.

The first to get hit was Hank the Bank, a Persico soldier with narcolepsy. He fell asleep at the wheel of his car and two of Vic's guys blew his head off. Rosario Nastasa aka Cut 'em Up Sam or Black Sam, an old-timer since the days of Profaci, considered himself neutral. He was playing cards in his social club when Persico guys walked in and shot him. Johnny Minerva, an original Persico guy who switched sides to join Vic, was killed outside his home along with his neighbor, a civilian who Minerva was speaking with. Many civilians and non-made men were killed in that war.

Salvatore "Big Fat Sal" Miciotta switched sides and went to Vic. One day, Persico guys pull up to a club on Avenue U owned by Nicky Black Grancio, a captain with Vic's faction. Standing outside, they fired their weapons into the club. Nicky Black wasn't even there, instead Tommy Scar Amato, a made man in his seventies with the Genovese Family, was accidentally killed. (Nicky Black was killed later in the war. He was shot while sitting behind the wheel of a car in January 1992.)

The Persicos, worried over this mistake, reached out to the Genovese people. The Persicos emphatically apologized, offered to pay for the funeral services, and compensate Tommy Scar's family with money. The Genovese Family responded, "Straighten out your problems. We're gonna put this on the back burner, for now."

Meanwhile, Carmine Sessa, a Persico loyalist, became acting consigliere with Teddy Persico, Junior's brother, in the background calling the shots. Sessa had an appointment to meet with Teddy at St. Patrick's Cathedral, but instead the FBI showed up and arrested him on murder charges.

At the same time, in Vic's camp, Big Fat Sal Miciotta began cooperating with the feds. The Colombo Family members were not only in a bloody war with one another, but both sides were now fighting a war with the feds.

As a result of those men cooperating with authorities, federal indictments came down. Vic Orena, Patty Amato, and a bunch of guys got indicted on a case. Wild Bill and ten members of his crew got indicted on another case. On the Persico side, Chucky Russo, Jo Jo Russo, and Joe Monte got indicted on a third case. During the indictments, Little Allie Boy, Junior's son, returned from prison. It was 1994, and he quickly took the reins of the Persico faction.

The first to go to trial were Wild Bill and his men. Wild Bill picked a top lawyer for himself and told all of his men to pick any lawyer, except his, and that he would pay for their legal defense.

In the middle of the trial, Wild Bill's defense team discovered that Greg Scarpa, a Persico captain, was in bed with the feds at the same time he was murdering people. Once the jury heard that, Wild Bill and his men were acquitted. Vic and the men on the other cases used a similar defense as Wild Bill, but with no success. They all received life sentences instead.

After Wild Bill beat his case, he met with Little Allie Boy to straighten out their differences. He gave Little Allie Boy $400,000 owed to the Persicos before the war. Now, with Wild Bill going back to the Persicos with all of his men, the tide shifted. The Persicos had most of the men except sixteen holdouts from Vic's side. Little Allie Boy became the boss, Joel "Joe Waverly" Cacace became the consigliere, and Wild Bill became the underboss. A cease fire was agreed upon. However, the sixteen holdouts were doing their own thing.

One of the rules in the Mafia is that every made man has to be under a captain, under a ruling administration. Independents, or men trying to operate on their own, are considered outlaws, which is unacceptable.

To prevent war from reigniting, Little Allie Boy met with Frank "Farby" Serpico, the acting boss of the Genovese Family, for assistance in bringing the sixteen holdouts back into the fold. Farby suggested that Little Allie Boy bring a proposal to the other faction to entice them back. He said, "Joe Colombo Sr. was the boss of the family. Maybe you should offer his son, Joe Colombo Jr. the number two spot. You get along with Joe and this way the other side has true representation."

Little Allie Boy agreed to meet with them at the Manhattan Cafe on 64th Street and 1st Avenue. Joe Colombo Jr., Jimmy Brown Clemenza, and Frankie Melli were waiting outside of the restaurant to meet with the Persicos and hear their propositions.

Tommy Gioeli, a Colombo captain and longtime Persico loyalist pulled up in a car and told the three men to get in. The men refused. "This wasn't the arrangement. We're supposed to meet in the restaurant."

Tommy was arrogant. "We'll take you where we want to take you," he said.

It seemed to the three men that the Persicos did not have good intentions. Even if they were not going to attempt to take the men out and were serious about negotiating for Joe Jr. to have the number two spot, they shouldn't have acted that way. Maybe they just wanted to show their dominance and that they were in power. However, the three men refused to submit and the meeting that was supposed to take place fell apart.

The three men returned to the Genovese people and told them what had happened.

The Genovese people were disgusted at what the Persicos had attempted to do. It was difficult to set up a meeting, so Farby plainly stated, "Now these guys can go fuck themselves."

Farby and the Genovese Family were not going to jeopardize their freedom by meeting directly with any of the members of either faction of the Colombo Family. When the top men of families meet, it is too often a serious danger because the fed's radar zeroes in. The Genovese felt they had provided an opportunity for a peaceful solution, but that opportunity was lost to the Persicos' arrogance.

Around this time, Joe Massino, the official boss of the Bonanna Family, returned home from prison. Once he returned, he called for a Commission meeting. The bosses and representatives present at this meeting were Massino; Pete Gotti, boss of the Gambino Family; Louie Daidone, acting boss of the Lucchese Family; Farby, acting boss of the Genovese Family; and Joe Waverly, representing the Colombo Family.

Little Allie Boy was not present because he had been arrested on a gun possession charge while on vacation in Florida. At that meeting in 1996, the Commission officially recognized Little Allie Boy as the acting boss of the Colombo Family. It was also decided at that meeting to allow the Colombos to straighten out five new members.

After this Commission meeting, an emissary from the Genovese Family was sent to meet with Frankie Melli and Paul "Paulie Guns" Bevacqua, giving a clear message that all of the families are recognizing Little Allie Boy as the official boss of the Colombo Family. The emissary said, "We would like all of you fella's to come back into the fold, or you're gonna have problems with all of the families, not just the Persicos."

The next day, eleven of the sixteen holdouts came back and pledged allegiance to the Persico regime. The five members that refuse to come back—Anthony Colombo, Joseph Colombo Jr., Vinny Aloi, and Jerry and Jimmy Brown Clemenza—knew they would not be treated fairly under that regime.

When Joe Colombo Sr. passed away, he left a building he personally owned on 86th Street in Brooklyn to his sons. The Persicos made them sell the building and took all of the money from the sale. Kaplan Buick Car Dealership, paying shakedown protection money, was also handed down to the Colombo sons. When the Persicos took over, they pushed aside the two sons again. Anthony and Joe Jr. were promised a portion of the monthly payments and a new car every two years, which the Persicos never honored. When a new regime takes over they clean house.

The Persicos did everything they were supposed to do by pushing aside the old regime in a proper manner and taking what had become theirs. Anthony and Joe Jr. felt that the building was given to them by their father and had nothing to do with business.

With lingering resentments, and having their own money and wealth, those made men actually responded to the emissary with, "We don't care who the Commission puts as boss, we would fall in line. But we refuse to be under the Persico rule."

Most of those five guys had substantial fortunes. They were known as "big money guys." They took a big risk by holding out, even though it was the wisest of moves. The Commission never allowed for made men to leave the life with their lives. The families were no longer allowed to recognize those men or do business with them.

Because everyone was tired of the violence and the heat from the government, the decision was made not to kill those men. In the past it not only would have been suggested, but quickly carried out. One of the rules is that you are not allowed to just leave. Regardless of the circumstances of those situations and the continued warring, it set a bad precedent. In the Mafia, rules should always be followed, no exceptions.

Little Allie Boy pled on the gun charge and got eighteen months. Joe Waverly and Wild Bill ran the family with Tom Gioeli as acting boss. Another wise move was that all family matters and business went through Wild Bill to keep the spotlight off of the acting boss while holding onto the Persico rule and power, or so it seemed.

During that period, the feds got a tip and found shylock records in a Bay Ridge, Brooklyn apartment implicating Little Allie Boy. He got transferred to Metropolitan Detention Center with another case for extortion.

Seeing that Little Allie Boy would be incarcerated even longer with new federal charges—he got thirteen years in 2001 for racketeering, loan-sharking, and money laundering—Wild Bill decided to take over the family. He planned to knock off Gioeli and Waverly, but as Colombo Family history shows, whoever he trusted with his plan gave him up.

Wild Bill arrived for a regular monthly meeting in Dino "Little Dino" Saracino's basement apartment with Gioeli, Little Dino, and Dino "Big Dino" Calabro. Everyone was seated when Big Dino got up to for a coffee and shot Wild Bill in the head. They wrapped him up and buried him.

After Wild Bill, the top Persico men were fed up with placing power guys up front only to have them try to take over the family. Therefore, they placed Sally Fusco, son of Dick Fusco, a well-respected soldier with Joe Colombo Sr., in the position. Sally was a low-level wiseguy who they elevated to captain and placed as acting boss. Gioeli remained behind the scenes, Waverly was consigliere, and Jack DeRoss became the acting under boss.

After Wild Bill disappeared, DeRoss brought all the men in and informed them that he was the guy. DeRoss was with Junior from day one and was incarcerated for six years during the last war. He inherited all of Wild Bill's men and earnings. Everything of Wild Bill's went to him.

Within a year, things fell apart. Sally Fusco died of a heart attack. DeRoss was arrested for racketeering and joined Little Allie Boy in prison. In 2004, Waverly was arrested and copped to twenty years in prison. Joseph "Joe Campy" Campanella, a soldier under Wild Bill, got arrested for attempted murder and flipped for the government. Wild Bill's son wore a wire implicating Little Allie Boy and DeRoss in his father's murder. The two men got indicted with the first trial ending in a hung jury. At the second trial in 2007 they were convicted. Little Allie Boy and DeRoss each got life sentences.

Joseph "Joey Caves" Competiello, a Colombo associate around Big Dino and Little Dino, got arrested and was held without bail. He cooperated with the feds and gave up the Wild Bill murder. According to his testimony, in Little Dino's basement, Gioeli and the two Dinos were there when Big Dino shot Bill. He testified that he helped them wrap and bury the body. The feds indicted Gioeli and the two Dinos and held them without bail. Big Dino, the supposed shooter, turned rat. The government had an airtight case. The Colombo Family was in disarray.

As I've explained, you must have clear plans with every detail accounting for all possibilities if you are to gain power and hold on to that power in the Mafia.

The Persicos showed great qualities of made men with clear plans and precision in their execution of those plans. They held power from the moment they became the ruling regime. Since the death of Profaci, the original boss of that family, there had been rampant betrayal and treachery with many vying for the top spots, which the Persicos had always been an intricate part of. But in the era of the rat, the Persicos and Colombo Family not only had to contend with treachery and betrayal, but with the feds also.

Junior's first cousin, Andrew Russo, had been a captain in the family since the 1980s. When he returned from prison in 2010, he took the reins of the Colombo Family and tried to put things back together. He made Benny Castellazzo the underboss and Ritchie Fusco the consigliere. As he pieced together what the government and the rats had destroyed, he was unaware that he had to contend with rats. It was always evident that anyone in a life of crime, especially the Mafia, had to contend and guard against the government and their many resources, which were directed at them for the purpose of completely destroying the life.

Anyone in the life, especially the top guys, must always maintain a low profile and take precautions to stay off the government's radar. The true boss of the family should always remain behind the scenes and not interact with the soldiers, not even with the captains, which the Persicos had always been adept at doing by putting figurehead bosses up front.

However, with the family in disarray, Andrew Russo worked for the continuation of their organization and their hold on that power. He had to deal with the captains. There wasn't enough time, or enough solid men, to put together the ruling administration with the needed safety factors.

So, Andrew Russo came home unknowingly to Paulie Guns, a captain who had been wearing a wire since 2006; to Anthony "Big Anthony" Russo, a captain from Staten Island who is not related to Andrew, wearing a wire; and to Reynold Maragni, another captain, wearing a wire. It is impossible for a family to function when there are three captains wearing a wire for the very organization that is trying to destroy the family. Associates, soldiers, captains, and especially the boss of the family are in a no-win situation.

Maragni was a high-ranking captain who was trying to hold the family together until Andrew Russo returned from prison. He met a soldier in the Staten Island Mall while wearing a wire and asked, "How did everything go with the Bill hit?"

It has always been a rule to never talk about someone who was murdered with anyone else, regardless of rank in the family. However, the soldier, a subordinate of Maragni's, gave him the details that went directly into the government wire.

Again, the top administration of the Colombo Family was wiped out, perhaps for the last time. Throughout the history of the Colombo Family, betrayal, treachery, and warring among its own members had diminished its effectiveness as a properly functioning crime family.

The Persicos always did what they were supposed to do to seize power and hold on to it. They followed the rules and their predecessor's playbook. However, when there is too much violence, murder, and warring, there are too many obstacles for even the greatest and most detailed plans.

One of the biggest obstacles is the US government, the most powerful law enforcement agency in the world. It has unlimited resources and is determined to destroy the Mafia.

The Genovese Family members, unlike most families, do not war among themselves and properly follow the rules and protocols set down through the generations. That has allowed them to continue to thrive as the most powerful Mafia family. They interact with the other families as little as possible.

Although Junior and his son, Little Allie Boy, are in prison for life, they remain the Colombo Family's boss and acting boss. In January 2011, Colombo street boss, Andrew Russo, along with Richard "Ritchie Nerves" Fusco and Benjamin "Benny" Castellazzo were arrested and charged with murder, drug trafficking, and labor racketeering. Fusco and Castellazzo pleaded guilty to reduced charges. Russo, seventy-eight, was sentenced to thirty-three months for racketeering, but because of his age and medical ailments he was released in 2013.

In a January 30, 2011 New York Post article on the arrests that decimated the Colombo ranks, one law-enforcement source said, "They did it to themselves," noting that a parade of well-placed informants had systemically sold out their fellow mobsters since 2005. "The Colombos can still draw on veteran mafiosi like longtime boss Carmine Persico, who continues to call the shots from jail, but there's just one Persico relative who is not in prison or dead, Danny Persico, a minor figure who lives on Long Island. Everyone else is six feet under or locked up. There's nobody left," said a veteran investigator. "The old-timers are too old and too tired. There are still big money-makers who bring in tons of cash, but they're not combatants. They are not involved in homicides. To run things, you need somebody who has two sides to him."

Chapter Ten

Cardinal Rule

Bartholomew "Bobby" Boriello grew up in Brooklyn. He lived on Henry Street near Carroll Street. He was a kind of guy you had to like. He started out with the Gallo brothers, who were based on President Street between Columbia and Van Brunt streets.

After years of turmoil and war between the Gallos and Colombos, Bobby joined the Genovese Family as an associate. But after a few years, Bobby wanted to go on his own and asked the Genovese Family to release him. At that point, Bobby didn't want to be with any crew or family. So, he stood by himself.

Bobby and a friend opened a Chock full o' Nuts coffee shop on Bay Parkway and 86th Street. His friend did well with the coffee shop and took care of Bobby.

One day, Bobby stopped by the shop and his friend told him, "Someone threw a brick through the window." He showed Bobby the brick and boarded-up front window. His friend said to Bobby, "I think it was someone from the club around the corner. They are always asking me for money for protection."

Bobby took the brick and went to the club, which was located over a bakery. He walked in and said, "Whoever threw this brick through the coffee shop on the corner tell them I'm going to tie it around their neck and throw them in the ocean."

An old man got up and said to Bobby, "Do you know who I am?" Bobby said, "I don't care. If all of you want trouble, go in the coffee shop again." Bobby walked out. After Bobby checked around, he learned the old guy was Pat Lori, a made member of the Gambino Family. So Bobby took a ride out to Queens to see his friend John Gotti.

Both Bobby and John did time in the state pen together. Bobby walked in John's club, the Bergen Hunt and Fish Club in Ozone Park. John got up and hugged and kissed Bobby. "What's up, pal?" John asked. Bobby told Gotti the story. John said, "I'll take care of this. You have a disadvantage; this guy's made and you're not."

A few days later, Bobby's friend asked him to visit the coffee shop. When Bobby got there, his friend said, "The guy around the corner wants to see you."

Bobby went to meet him. When he walked in, Pat Lori put out his hand. Bobby shook it. Pat said, "Hey listen, Bobby, it was a big misunderstanding. It won't happen again. If you need me for anything, just come up. My club is your club."

Bobby thanked Pat and left. That week, on a Wednesday night, Bobby drove to Queens where John Gotti had dinner with his guys on Wednesdays. Bobby walked in with a case of champagne for John. John said, "Bobby, you didn't have to do this."

Bobby said, "I wanted to."

John said, "Okay, have dinner with us."

Bobby stayed for dinner with John and his crew. There were twenty-five guys. Bobby knew most of them, especially Angelo Ruggiero. After dinner, Bobby said to John, "Do you think we can take a walk? I would like to talk to you."

Bobby told John, "I would really like to be over here with you."

John said, "It's the best news I've heard all month. I'll have to ask O'Neil to go and talk with the Genovese people so there isn't any problem later."

After two weeks, John invited Bobby to Wednesday dinner, but to come an hour earlier than everyone else. When Bobby arrived, John Gotti and Angelo Ruggiero were waiting for him. John said, "It's official. You are now with us." It was all hug and kisses.

Later after dinner, John broke the news to the rest of the crew. Everyone was happy to have Bobby as part of the crew. Bobby was a tough guy and the kind of man John Gotti had in mind. He needed all the tough guys he could get.

Eddie Lino grew up in the Gravesend part of Brooklyn. Eddie was a real tough guy in the late '70s early '80s. He stood with a very rough crew of guys, including Ciro, "Ruby" Rabino, Georgie "Crowbar," Charlie LaRocca, and a couple of others. They all sold and used drugs. At night they would meet at a bar on Avenue T and West 7th Street in Brooklyn called the Wrong Number Lounge. There they would get all juiced up, mostly on cocaine, then go out clubbing. God help you if you crossed paths with them.

There was a disco in Manhattan were some of them would go. I was there one night when Eddie and Ciro came in. If girls walked by the bar where Eddie and Ciro were drinking and the girls were good looking, Eddie or Ciro would just grab one by the arm, "Come and have a drink with us." They didn't care if a girl was with a guy.

Both of them carried guns at all times and both were very good with their hands. So one night they grabbed a girl who was walking by with her boyfriend. When the guy opened his mouth, he got kicked and punched out the door. As the guy stood outside thinking what to do, I went out to him and said, "I know what I am going to say is hard, but just go home; your girlfriend will be fine. I've seen this happen before. They won't hurt her, but they will hurt you. So just go home."

A couple of Eddie's crew would go into bars in Brooklyn late at night, start fights and wreck the bars, not caring who owned them. One night, Georgie "Crowbar" and Charlie LaRocca went to an after-hours club on 86th Street in Brooklyn. After a while, Georgie and Charlie pulled out guns and shot them in the air. Everyone was in shock. There were two girls working as barmaids. Georgie and Charlie told them to strip naked and go down on each other or they would shoot them. They hit some of the customers, then wrecked the place and left.

About a month later, Georgie and Charlie were found in the back of a van wrapped up in rugs, both shot dead. Six month after that, Ciro was found beaten up bad and shot a couple of times in the head.

One thing about Eddie Lino, none of his crew had any respect for wiseguys or guys in the life, but Eddie had a very good relationship with the underboss of the Gambino Family, Mr. O'Neil Dellacroce. The next one to go was Ruby Rabino. He was found dead in his car. So, Eddie thought it would be a good time to go on record with Mr. O'Neil Dellacroce and the Gambino Family. That's what happened. After that, if anyone had any ideas of killing Eddie, they would have to deal with Mr. O'Neil and the Gambino Family.

Through Mr. O'Neil and his Ravenite Club, Eddie Lino got very close with John Gotti and his Queens crews. He got into the heroin business with Angelo Ruggiero and the others, and was arrested with them.

It was late 1985. The Gambino Family had troubles. Mr. O'Neil Dellacroce was dying of cancer. Paul Castellano was facing the Commission case and the stolen car ring case. Paul's trusted captain, Nino Gaggi, had died of a heart attack. It happened while he was in a Brooklyn jail waiting for his case to come up.

And the tapes the feds got from wiretapping Ruggiero's house were causing problems between Paul and Gotti's crew. Paul kept telling a sick Mr. O'Neil that he wanted the tapes, and Mr. O'Neil, housebound where the feds had also placed a bug, would send for Gotti and Ruggiero. He told them to give Paul the tapes, and he would stand behind them.

Ruggiero was like a son to Mr. O'Neil, but he would say, "Forget it. I'm not giving Paul anything." At that time, John Gotti's plan to take control of the family was already in the works, but if Mr. O'Neil knew what John had in mind, he would never have agreed to it. John knew Mr. O'Neil didn't have much longer to live, so he would just wait. On Dec. 2, 1985, Mr. O'Neil passed away. They had a wake for him at Guiddetti Funeral Home on Spring Street between Mott and

Mulberry streets in Little Italy, right around the block from Mr. O'Neil's Ravenite Social Club.

He lay in wake there for two days, but neither Paul nor Tommy Bilotti showed up. Paul said it was too hot with the feds and other law enforcement around. Gotti was mad. He said to a bunch of us standing around, "Were the flowers too hot to send, too?" John said Mr. O'Neil should have been the boss after Carlo Gambino died, but being the man he was, Mr. O'Neil stepped aside for Paul. Mr. O'Neil was the underboss of the family for thirty years and Paul could not show respect by coming to the wake.

Five days after Mr. O'Neil died Paul called a meeting with Gotti and the other captains. At this meeting, Paul named Bilotti his underboss to replace Mr. O'Neil. Paul also gave Bilotti all of Mr. O'Neil's rackets and earnings. Big mistake.

Paul should have played it differently. First, he should have made Bilotti and a couple of his men show up at Mr. O'Neil's wake to show Mr. O'Neil and Gotti some respect. Second, Paul should have made John the underboss until Paul could put a plan together to see how he was going to deal with John and his crew over the drugs. I'm sure at that point he didn't have to listen to any tapes. Paul wanted them, but never got them.

Paul needed to outthink John because Paul couldn't outfight him. Mr. O'Neil and his side of the Gambino Family were the muscle. Mr. O'Neil had all the tough guys. Paul was at a big loss of strength with Nino Gaggi dead and Frankie DeCicco going against him. So a smart boss would have thought like a fox, would have outsmarted them. But Paul had no fox in him.

Mr. O'Neil was the only thing that came between Gotti and his plan. Once Mr. O'Neil was gone, John wasn't going to wait around to see what Paul had on his mind. Paul Castellano let his guard down and he would pay for it with his life.

On Dec. 16, 1985, Paul and Bilotti were on their way to Sparks Steakhouse in Manhattan to meet DeCicco, Jimmy Brown Failla, and a couple of others. When Paul and Tommy pulled up in front, they were met with a hit team. Both were killed.

In the Mafia, you can't kill an official boss, and you, especially, can't kill a boss without the other bosses giving an okay. The reason is if one group gets away with killing a boss, any crew in any family can do it too.

John Gotti did what it takes to take control of a family. He followed through on his plan. He was decisive. But John Gotti broke a cardinal rule: he killed a boss.

Chapter Eleven

Gotti the Boss

John Gotti had no choice but to act once Mr. O'Neil was gone and Paul Castellano had made Tommy Bilotti underboss. John's future in the Gambino Family would have been over if he hadn't made the move.

As underboss, Bilotti would have broken Gotti down to soldier and broken up his crew, spreading them out under captains Paul trusted once Angelo Ruggerio and the others were convicted of drug dealing. Paul might have had John killed, who knows.

Now with Paul and Bilotti gone, John and Frankie DeCicco called in the captains and John told them, "We are going to find out what happened to Paul and Tommy, so for now just sit tight. Right now any problems or troubles you have you come to me or Frankie."

When Gotti and DeCicco showed the rest of the captains they were running the family, Joe N. Gallo, the consigliere, the only one left from the Castellano administration, stood right next to them.

In the next few weeks, the feds were all over Gotti. It spread like wild fire that John killed Paul. John had his men around him at all times, not knowing who would move against him. Because he broke the rules, it could have been one of the other families or all of the other families that would move on him. One way or another, the price for killing Paul would have to be paid.

In the middle of January 1986, Joe N. Gallo called a meeting with all the captains. At the meeting Gallo said, "I pick John Gotti as the official boss of the Gambino Family." DeCicco stood up and said, "I second it." John, now the official boss, stood up and said, "For my underboss, I pick Frankie DeCicco." Then John said, "And Joe Gallo will stay on as our consigliere."

Gotti's next move was to get the blessing of all the other families since his killing of Paul without getting approval from the Commission broke the cardinal rule. Gotti knew he wouldn't have any problems with the Bonannos or the Colombos. Joe Massino was the Bonanno boss and John's good friend. He was in prison, but had his brother-in-law, Sally Vitale, the underboss, going to John whenever he needed advice. It was the same with the Colombo Family. Little Vic Orena, who Junior Persico made acting boss in 1988, would go to John too.

The family John worried about was the biggest, and the one that could really hurt him: the Genovese Family. Fat Tony Salerno was the street boss, but behind the scenes the real boss was Vincent "Chin" Gigante.

An appointment was made with Chin. Joe N. Gallo argued that John Gotti was their boss and DeCicco the underboss. Chin wished all of them luck, though he knew exactly what had happened to Paul and Tommy and would never tip his hand. This was a real boss, smart as a whip. So for the moment, he went along with the program.

The other family that could have given John trouble was the Luccheses. A much smaller family than Genovese or Gambino, the Lucchese's leaders, Vic and Anthony "Gaspipe" Casso, were no nonsense guys. So they gave their approval, too.

Even though all the families accepted Gotti as boss of the Gambino Family, John had to watch his back because smart bosses will rock you to sleep.

Now it was time for Gotti and DeCicco to call in the captains and big earners to see what sort of money would be coming to them. The first two wiseguys that were sent for were Robert "DB" DiBernardo, who was a big earner and answered right to Paul, and Sammy the Bull Gravano. Louie Milito would have been there with Gravano, but Louie was in prison for loan-sharking. Gravano was in charge of all the construction.

At that meeting, DeCicco said, "If it's okay with you, John, I would like to take down Toddo Aurello and make Sammy captain of the crew. He handles all the construction and our interest with all the other families." If Louie was home it could have been him who got that spot. But Gravano was there and he got it. So when Louie came home from prison, he was under Gravano and didn't mind. It was business as usual.

By then Gravano and Louie had $1 million on the streets collecting. And they still had their own construction company. After everything was in order, Gotti and DeCicco couldn't believe the money that was coming in. DeCicco said to one of his men, "If me and John just get a two-year run, we won't know where to put the money."

DeCicco never had big money. He lived well, but gambling kept him down. Now, in March 1986, he was the underboss of one of the biggest crime families in New York City. He was in the best shape of his life. DeCicco was one of the nicest, good-hearted men you would ever find in organized crime. Especially as an underboss, DeCicco was for the underdog. So Gambino Family members would have done well with DeCicco as the underboss.

But on April 13, 1986, the first blow against Gotti and DeCicco for killing Paul Castellano came. John had made his first mistake as the boss by how he took over the Gambino Family—killing a boss without the Commission's approval.

His next mistake was falling into a routine. As a boss, you never fall into a routine. Every Sunday John would come from Queens with a couple of his men and Frankie would come from Staten Island with a couple of his men. They would meet at Jimmy Brown Failla's club on 86th Street in Brooklyn, the Veterans and Friends Social Club. They would stay there a couple of hours, talk and have some coffee. Then, John and DeCicco would get into DeCicco's black Buick Electra and they would drive together to Manhattan to the Ravenite Social Club, Mr. O'Neil Dellacroce's old place. This was every Sunday, so it was easy to put a bomb under DeCicco's car. They were looking to get both John and DeCicco together.

One Sunday John didn't show up. He was sick. But once the bomb was in place, they had to set it off. DeCicco came out of the club with Frankie Hearts, a Lucchese wiseguy, to give him a phone number he had in the car. Once DeCicco sat in the front seat, the bomb went off killing him and blowing Frankie Hearts away from the car.

Everyone thought Gotti was behind DeCicco's death, because in the four months he was boss Gotti had built an army of men. Also, John and DeCicco were partners who didn't always agree. DeCicco let John have the top spot only because of John's ego. But if DeCicco thought he was right on an issue, he would stand up to John.

Once, when they were planning a trip to Florida, John told DeCicco to leave for Florida at another time. DeCicco said to John, "I'm going at that same time, and I already booked everything." John, as the boss, thought DeCicco should have canceled. But DeCicco, as a partner and equal, didn't.

With DeCicco gone, no one in the Gambino Family would ever stand up to John. But after DeCicco's death, John made the biggest mistake of his life. He picked Gravano as his underboss. John should have left him as a captain and picked one of his guys from Queens for the job. All the money Sammy was bringing in would have continued to come in.

Once Gravano became underboss, he had to pick one of his men to take over his crew. Everyone thought it would have been his best friend, Louie Milito, but he picked a guy who had been made two years earlier.

Louie was fit to be tied. He couldn't believe Sammy would do that to him. Louie let Gravano know just how he felt. Some people would like it to be known that Louie betrayed Gravano, but it was the other way around. Now that Gravano was Mister Big, he didn't need his best friend anymore, so he kept telling John that Louie was disrespecting him, talking to the men wrong, and telling stories about him. None of that was true. After bothering John enough about it, Gravano got the okay to kill his best friend, the man who'd saved his life and the reason Gravano was a Gambino.

John Gotti as boss should have been sharp enough to look at what his underboss was trying to do. But with all the bags of money Gravano was bringing in, John let Gravano do whatever he wanted. On March 8, 1988, Louie disappeared. Gravano took over the construction company they owned together. He kept all the street money. He told Louie's wife, "It would be better if you and your kids moved to Florida." Louie and his wife owned a used car lot in Staten Island. Gravano took it.

Sometimes we as men make mistakes, and we should correct them right away. But when it's all about the money we push all our principles aside. Gotti made another mistake as boss. He removed Joe N. Gallo as consigliere. Joe had taken John and DeCicco around to the other families after Paul Castellano was killed and backed them as boss and underboss.

With all the respect Joe had gained after all the years he was Carlo Gambino's consigliere and all his experience with the other families, Joe deserved better. Gotti replaced him with Joe "Piney" Armone, a real good man, but not a Joe N. Gallo. In 1988, Gallo went to prison for bribery. After his release seven years later, he died of a broken heart.

When Gravano was a captain, he and Louie DiBono had a big problem over money from a construction job they did. DiBono was a made member of the Gambino Family and happened to be right, so Gravano got the short end of it.

When Gotti sent for DiBono with Gravano as the new underboss, Louie was afraid to come in. So what do you do? You kill DiBono. This was the new way to settle things in the Gambino Family. This was John Gotti's way.

Robert "DB" DiBernardo was a very big earner in the Gambino Family. He was the biggest in the pornography business. He was a made man and answered only to Paul Castellano. He also had an interest in a lot of discos on Long Island. He wasn't in the muscle end of the family. He was no threat to John Gotti.

When you want to kill someone who didn't do anything wrong, you as the underboss sit with your boss and consigliere and make up reasons why this person should be killed. So, one day when DB went to see Gravano at his construction company on Stillwell Avenue in Brooklyn he was never seen again. All of DB's earnings were taken over. Most of it went to John Gotti.

John often didn't conduct himself as a boss should. One afternoon, in September 1984 when he was a Gambino captain, John was in a restaurant in Manhattan. He was double-parked out front. When he came out, a refrigerator repairman, who was blocked in by John's car, started mouthing off. One of John's guys punched him, but then John gave the repairman a slap in the face so hard he almost broke the guy's nose. Could you picture Carlo Gambino slapping a guy like that?

Of course, the repairman went and got the cops, and John was arrested for assault. On March 24, 1986, when the case came up for trial (and by this time John was the Gambino boss), Romual Piecyk, the repairman, well aware of who John Gotti was, couldn't remember what the guy who slapped him looked like. The judge threw the case out.

People believe that when John Gotti became the boss he started to wear expensive suits, but John always dressed well and always dined out with his men. When John took over the Gambino Family, he should have lowered his exposure a little, especially with all the heat he was getting from the feds. Instead, he got worse. He had all his men report to him every Wednesday night at the Ravenite Social Club on Mulberry Street. This was plain crazy to expose all the members of his family. Everyone knew how much John hated the feds, so why make it easy for them?

But every Wednesday night the feds just set up shop on Mulberry Street and they took pictures, collected plate numbers, and recorded sound if they could get any. Soldiers showed up that the feds didn't even know were in the family. Then, every Saturday, all John's captains had to report to him in Queens at his Bergin Hunt and Fish Club.

The captains didn't like showing up. They complained, but not to John because they were afraid of getting killed. This was the late 1980s, not the 1950s, but John came in as boss with a loud bang and kept banging.

⌒Chapter Twelve⌒

GOTTI AND GRAVANO

On the west side of Lower Manhattan, right outside the Brooklyn-Battery Tunnel, there was a restaurant called Bankers and Brokers. It was 1986 and the owner was an old-time Gambino wiseguy named Philly Modica. He lost his lease on the restaurant and moved across the street to Battery Park.

He started to rebuild the new restaurant using nonunion workers. When the business agent of Local 608 of the Carpenters Union, a guy named John O'Connor, found out, he sent a couple of guys to break the place up. They hadn't checked to see if anyone was connected.

When the story reached John Gotti, he blew his top right there in his club in Queens, which John had to know was bugged with the feds all over him. It was actually a state-organized task force that was listening as John told a crew, "You have to bust him up. Put a rocket in his pocket."

So the Westies, the Irish gang that ran Hell's Kitchen on the west side of Manhattan and worked with the Gambino Family, are hired. They shoot O'Connor in the ass, leg, and hip while he was in his office. He recovered and would testify in court. As the boss, Gotti should have let men under him handle that. That's why he had an underboss and a consigliere.

On January 23, 1989, with the state prosecutor working off the state task force tape of Gotti ordering O'Connor shot, John and Anthony "Tony Lee" Guerrieri were arrested for the shooting. John found a way to pay off one of the jurors, who in turn convinced the rest of the jurors to go with a not guilty verdict. If the jury had found him guilty, John would have been done.

In the Commission case, all the bosses of the Five Families got caught with their pants down. Law enforcement had never gone after all the bosses at once, but this time they had wiretap evidence. This was February 1985.

First, Paul Castellano held court every Sunday in his house, which was bugged. He talked about everything. Next, Tony Ducks Corallo, the Lucchese Family boss, talked in his bugged Jaguar. He talked about Commission meetings and when they were scheduled. Genovese Family street boss, Fat Tony Salerno's club on 116th Street and 1st Avenue was bugged.

Then an underboss from Cleveland got arrested for drug dealing and decided to wear a wire for the feds. He was eighty years old, so he went to see Fat Tony about problems he was having with the Teamsters union. Tony said on tape, "I'll have to bring this problem in front of the other bosses at the next Commission meeting." It was all on tape. When the trial of the bosses came up in September 1986, they were dead.

Out of desperation, the bosses decided to let Colombo boss, Junior Persico, defend himself. They felt that Junior could ask the cooperating witnesses questions that their lawyers couldn't, but Junior wasn't sure. He said, "We are at a big disadvantage. I can't ask a person who is in prison to come and testify and tell them, 'I'll get you out for time served' or 'Testify for us and I'll put you in witness protection.'"

Of course, it didn't work. On November 19, 1986, the bosses—the Genovese's Fat Tony Salerno, Colombo's Carmine "Junior" Persico, Lucchese's Anthony "Tony Ducks" Corallo—and five underbosses, consiglieres, and soldiers were convicted. The bosses each received hundred-year sentences as did one Colombo soldier, Ralph Scopo.

Nearly a year before the trial began, defendant Aniello "Mr. O'Neil" Dellacroce, underboss of the Gambino Family, died of cancer and Gambino boss, Paul Castellano, was assassinated. Bonanno Family boss, Philip "Rusty" Rastelli, was severed from the case and tried under a different RICO case where he was convicted for labor racketeering and sentenced to twelve years. Except for Junior, all the bosses in the case have died. *Time* magazine called the Commission trial the "Case of Cases," prosecuted by then US Attorney Rudolph Giuliani, whose intent was "to wipe out the Five Families." He didn't wipe them out at the time; but eight years later, Giuliani would become mayor of New York City.

Gotti tried to consolidate power. He had Johnny D'Amato, the acting boss of New Jersey's DeCavalcante Family, under his wing. Sally Vitale, Bonanno Family acting boss, was going to him for advice. And Little Vic, the Colombo Family's acting boss, was meeting with John regularly. All of these families used to go to the Genovese people for advice. But once the feds put on the heat, the Genovese Family shut the door. So, with John as the new boss of the second largest crime family, that's where the other families went.

The Lucchese Family was in good shape, so they did their own thing. Gotti wanted to have Little Vic as the official boss of the Colombo Family and on his side. That would give John three votes on the Commission: himself, the Bonanno's Joe Massino, once he came home from prison, and Little Vic.

But no matter how many alliances John made, he always had the feeling that he had to pay for killing Paul, especially after DeCicco got blown up in his car.

On weeknights, John would surround himself with a few of his men. You would find him in a disco or a restaurant. His favorite disco was Club A, next to the 59th Street Bridge. Club A opened in the early '80s and closed down in the early '90s. The other club John liked was Regime's on Park Avenue. Only upper-class people would go there, but in the end, before Regime's closed down, it became a mob hang out. A lot of wiseguys from other families started hanging out there, especially when those wiseguys wanted to be around John Gotti.

The only night during the week that you might not see John around would be a Wednesday because he loved to play cards. The game was called Continental. It was gin played with jokers. Five or six could play to win the pot, though minus the cut, which was what the house would take out of every pot. They would change clubs every other Wednesday. It would be Joe Butcher's club then Jimmy Brown's club then John's club in Queens, so all the clubs could earn from the cut. The pots could be from $5,000 to $10,000. So the cut on $5,000 would be 10 percent, $500. With pots that size, the club could make $5,000 in a single night that would pay all the bills for the month and give a couple of guys that worked in the club good pay.

While all of this was going on, Gravano kept bringing John bags of money and a few contracts. There was a guy named Eddie Garofalo. He was in the demolition business. He did business with Gravano and his construction company. He always did the right thing by Gravano. When he had to kick money up, he did. But when Gravano learned the demolition business, he didn't need Eddie anymore. One night, Eddie won a Rolls Royce. Gravano wanted to buy it from him. Eddie politely told Gravano, "I really like it and want to keep it."

So now Gravano had it in for Eddie. He went to John and made up a lot of stories as to why they should kill Eddie. After a while, John gave Gravano the okay. So Eddie Garofalo got killed outside his house. Now, why kill a guy like Eddie? He wasn't a threat to John or Gravano, and he was a legitimate guy.

Another one of Gravano's contracts was his childhood friend, Nick "Nicky Cowboy" Mormando.

Gravano claimed Nicky was out of control. He went to John and told him Nicky was out of control on crack cocaine, and he knew too much. John gave Gravano the okay to kill Nicky. The only one who was out of control was Gravano.

The next contract was another friend of Gravano's, Michael "Mickey" DeBatt. Gravano told John he lost control of Mickey DeBatt and that he was on drugs and could hurt them. John gave Gravano the okay to kill him. So then his friend Mickey DeBatt got killed.

Gravano also wanted to kill his wife's brother, Nick Scibetta, who was gay. What could he have done? But Nick Scibetta got killed, though not on John's orders. Nick was killed in 1978 on Paul Castellano's orders.

What did all those guys do for the Gambino Family? Gravano had an army of wiseguys under him. He didn't need those guys to do anything for him. What was John Gotti thinking when Gravano kept bringing him all those contracts? Did all the money Gravano brought to John blind John so much that he let Gravano kill whoever he wanted to?

Any other boss of a family would have stopped Gravano cold. Right in the beginning they would have asked, "Sammy, where are we going with all these contracts?" Don't forget this was John Gotti's pick for the number two spot, his underboss of the Gambino Family. John put Gravano there, so how would it have looked to the rest of the family if John killed Gravano after his first underboss got blown up?

As all of this was going on, John and Gravano were making new members. For the Gambino Family, John brought his son John Jr., Bobby Boriello, and Eddie Lino. All became members of the Gambinos. Gravano brought in Mikey Scars DiLeonardo, Frank Fappiano, and Joe D'Angelo. Things were fine, but John had no idea what awaited him.

As I said before, John didn't know how to conduct himself like a boss. A Frank Sinatra story illustrates this. Frank started out singing with the Tommy Dorsey Band. He was under contract with Dorsey. So, as the story goes, when Frank wanted to go on his own and sing or be in a motion picture, he couldn't. The contract he'd signed was binding.

So Frank, who was born and raised in Hoboken, New Jersey, had a friend named Willie Moretti who at that time, the early 1940s, was a Genovese underboss. He ran the New Jersey part of the Genovese Family and hung out in a restaurant called Dukes. Willie met with Dorsey who, after Willie shoved a gun down his throat and threatened to kill him, released Sinatra from his contract.

After Willie's death in 1951, Frank remained close to the Genovese Family. They never wanted anything from Frank, just to sing on occasion at weddings or other affairs. Frank was an entertainer who had friends. One was Louie Dome Pacella, a Genovese wiseguy out of the Harlem crew. Louie Dome owned a restaurant in Manhattan called The Sprate Tables on 25th Street and 3rd Avenue. Frank would drop in from time to time. He also did a lot for the Genovese Family in Las Vegas, getting other entertainers to perform in hotels the family had an interest in.

One night in New York, Frank Sinatra and a couple of friends went to the St. Regis Hotel in Manhattan for a couple of drinks. When Frank went to the restroom, he walked by a table where John Gotti was sitting with a couple of his men.

When he came out of the restroom, he was met by two of Gotti's men who pushed Frank against the wall and told him, "The next time you see John Gotti you better come over and pay your respects to him. And by the way, you belong to him." Frank went over to John, shook his hand and apologized for not recognizing him.

The next day, Frank went to see his friend Louie Dome. He told Louie what happened and wanted to know what it was all about. Louie told him, "I'll take care of it."

Louie knew John well, so he went to see him. Now, Louie Dome was just a wiseguy in the Genovese Family, not a boss, so John outranked him. One of John's men said to Louie, "Do this the right way." Louie was a Harlem guy, so he went to see his captain. The captain brought the matter to the boss of the Genovese Family. The boss had a meeting with John. Frank Sinatra was never bothered again.

One day Gravano made a connection with a low-income housing project. When the bids went in, Gravano's company got the work. The first job was on Coney Island. It was about a hundred units. They went for a $125,000 each. Gravano would contract out the work he didn't want, like carpentry, aluminum siding, and brick work. Contractors had to have a wiseguy behind them in order to get the work when they put in their bids. They had to put in $100 a unit for Gravano and John. If the job was a hundred units, they had to bring in $10,000 dollars. One job in the Bronx was two hundred units. All the contractors would put $20,000 on top of their bids. The wiseguys behind the winning contractor would bring the money to Gravano.

Another business that popped up for the New York families was window replacements. The Genovese Family had the in. At the time, the whole city needed those windows. Pete Savino was a Genovese associate. He was the guy to go to for windows. He had an office on 100 Street in Brooklyn, between 3rd and 4th avenues.

Each family had a representative in the window business. Most meetings were held in Savino's office. Sometimes captains or even bosses would show up at these meetings because of the large amounts of money being made.

Before all of this, Savino was involved in untaxed cigarettes and drugs. He and Bobby Faransa were around a Genovese wiseguy named Gerard "Gerry" Pappa. These three guys killed two guys. One was a Colombo wiseguy, which wasn't good; the other a Colombo associate. The Genovese wiseguys killed Pappa in retaliation.

Savino was doing well with his windows business, but Faransa, a drug dealer, got arrested dealing to an undercover agent. Faransa decided to cooperate with the feds. He gave up Savino for the two murders. He took the feds to where the bodies were buried. So when the feds went after Savino they told him, "You give us all the window guys," which was all the wiseguys, "or you can go to prison for life."

Savino wore a wire. He let the feds bug the office where all the window meetings were held. Savino would create situations where everyone would have to get together in the bugged office. It was always about money. That always got everyone's attention.

With the bugs in place, everything said was on tape. The Lucchese's had a captain at those meetings, Peter "Fat Pete" Chiodo. The Colombos had their underboss, Benny Aloi. John Gotti had his brother Pete Gotti there once in a while. The Genovese underboss, Venero "Benny Eggs" Mangano, would be present.

All of those guys and a couple of others were arrested. Fat Pete Chido made a plea deal. Out on bail, Chiodo stopped at a gas station in Staten Island. Two gunmen jumped out of a car and shoot Chiodo twelve times. Chiodo was 6' and 350 pounds. He survived, and, of course, he cooperated with the feds. At the Windows trial everyone beat the charges except Benny Aloi and Benny Eggs. They each got fifteen years. Savino later died of cancer.

Chapter Thirteen

GOTTI FALLS

The Gambino Family always had a crew in Florida. One of the captains down there was Joe Paterno. He controlled Gambino interests in Miami and Fort Lauderdale. He was there for years. His hang out was a Chinese restaurant in the Thunderbird Hotel on Collins Avenue in Miami. Called Christen Lees, it had very good food and a big bar crowd.

Around 1986, Paterno and a couple of his men were arrested. So John Gotti sent for Paterno's acting captain, Augustus "Big Gus" Sclafani. Big Gus flew to New York. Gotti told Gus to hold down the fort until they saw what would happen to Paterno. In 1988, before Paterno could go to trial, he died from cancer.

John flew to Florida with a couple of his men. They met with Paterno's crew and Gotti made Eddie Lino captain and gave him the crew. Lino lived in New York, but he would make trips back and forth to Miami.

Then, in 1990, Lino was found shot dead in his car on the Belt Parkway near Brooklyn's Brighton Beach. Again, everyone thought John had ordered the hit. Lino was a captain and close to John, so everybody believed it came from John. But if John hadn't order the hits on Frankie DeCicco and Eddie Lino, who had? John must have been worrying, though he never showed it. You could still see John and his men out nights at Taormina's on Mulberry Street in Little Italy or Da Noi's on York Avenue, and at the discos, Club A or Regimes.

Shortly before Paul Castellano and Tommy Bilotti were killed on the night of December 16, 1985, they made a stop in Staten Island at a diner they always went to, the Country Club Diner. They met with John Riggi, the boss of the New Jersey DeCavalcante Family, regarding a business matter.

When the feds put the heat on the Genovese Family, they closed the door on most of the other families. So Paul took on the DeCavalcante Family, especially when he found out he could earn money with their construction business.

After Paul was killed, Riggi would check in with John Gotti and Gravano. They convinced Riggi to make Jimmy Rotondo, who had a position in the Brooklyn docks and the International Longshoremen's Association, his underboss. It made Riggi's job easier because Jimmy lived in Brooklyn, but it gave Gotti easy access to Jimmy.

Then Jimmy got killed for some unknown reason, and Riggi picked John "Johnny Boy" D'Amato for his new underboss. When Riggi got indicted by the feds and was held without bail, he made D'Amato acting boss of the DeCavalcante Family.

At that point D'Amato was checking in with Gotti. D'Amato loved the nightlife and had a gambling habit. He started to hang out with Gotti, who loved the idea of an acting boss of another family in his company. While hanging out with Gotti, D'Amato tried to keep up with him, but D'Amato was no match for Gotti's nightly gambling and spending. So he started to borrow money on points and began to owe bookmakers for bets he couldn't pay. He used up most of the family's money that belonged to Riggi. One day D'Amato disappeared.

Riggi made one of his captains, Vincent "Vinny Ocean" Palermo, acting boss. Vinny was a good earner, had plenty of money, and no bad habits. So, he got the reins of the DeCavalcante Family. But Vinny started making bad decisions. After Jimmy Rotondo's son, Anthony Rotondo, had a falling out with Anthony

Capo because of Capo's drug habit and violence, Vinny, to keep the peace, put Capo with him. Now Capo answered to the acting boss and learned much about what went on in the DeCavalcante Family.

Gotti and Sammy the Bull Gravano had a union delegate, Fred Weiss, who answered to them. They got word that Weiss was talking to the feds. So now they wanted to kill him. John Gotti and Gravano sent a hit team out to New Jersey where Fred Weiss lived, but the hit team came back and said it was too hard to get Weiss.

When Gotti and Gravano asked Vinny to help them kill Fred Weiss, Vinny jumped at the chance and Weiss was shot outside his house in 1989. When Gravano cooperated with the feds, one of the things he gave up was the Weiss hit, and a number of DeCavalcantes were indicted, including Vinny, Rotondo, Capo, and Jimmy Gallo who pulled the trigger on Weiss. The first to open up to the feds was Capo.

He hadn't made it to the federal building before he started to talk. Capo himself was involved in a couple of murders. Next, while held at the federal prison in Otisville, New York, Vinny, the acting boss, started cooperating. John Riggi was just about to get released from federal prison when he was indicted because of Vinny and Capo.

Riggi was at the Metropolitan Detention Center (MDC) on 29th Street in Brooklyn. He was eighty years old at that time. He was on the fourth floor and Anthony Rotondo was on the seventh floor. The only time they could see each other was Thursdays in chapel, which was the only day Christians are allowed to attend. One Thursday in chapel, Riggi sat next to Rotondo. He suspected Rotondo was about to turn for the feds, so he said, "Don't disgrace your father."

Needless to say, Riggi made a few mistakes putting the wrong guys in position in the DeCavalcante Family. He figured Rotondo out too late. Around Christmas 2001, at the MDC in Brooklyn, Rotondo left the seventh floor and started cooperating with the feds.

That left Jimmy Gallo, who pulled the trigger on Weiss. After all of those so-called men rolled over, what chance did Gallo have? At the age of fifty-eight, Gallo took a plea deal of twenty-five years. If he takes care of himself, he will be 80 when he comes out. Now that is a man.

As I said before, when you're born a man, nothing can turn you. But when you're born a rat, it only takes prison time to bring out your real colors. Riggi plead to ten years because of those three rats, Capo, Rotondo, and Vinny.

If Gotti had used his own men in the Weiss hit like he should have, the DeCavalante Family may not have had so much trouble. Eventually, all the Gambino soldiers involved with the Weiss hit got indicted anyway.

When the official bosses for a lot of the small families in New York went to prison, they made bad choices about which guys they put in charge. A lot of those guys under indictment rolled right over. As soon as the cuffs went on, they wanted to make deals for themselves, and they wanted to be with their wives and their kids. They should have stayed away from the crime business.

In 1988, Gambino men Joe "Piney" Armone and Joe N. Gallo both went to prison for ten years, convicted of racketeering. Piney passed away in prison; Gallo died shortly after his release from prison. They did not cooperate with the feds. They were men.

Left standing was John Gotti and Sammy the Bull Gravano. The number three spot was open. Gotti picked for his consigliere a Bronx captain, Frank "Frankie Loc" LoCascio. He was a good choice. Frankie Loc was a good earner, a low-key guy, and well respected in the Gambino Family. John should have picked Frankie Loc instead of Gravano when DeCicco got killed. A lot of guys would have remained alive and men wouldn't have gone to prison.

Gotti kept to his regular meetings on Wednesday nights at the Ravenite Social Club, where every once in a while he would meet his lawyers, Bruce Cutler and Jerry Shargel. That was another big mistake made by John. He should have met with them at the office or in a restaurant.

By that time, early 1990, John thought he was invincible. The feds couldn't get him. He had already beaten them in court a couple of times and now he was untouchable. The Colombo Family was getting ready to start killing each other, again. Bonanno Family boss, Joe Massino, John's good friend, had come home. Joe couldn't move around because he had three years supervised release. His brother-in-law, Sally Vitale, was still holding down the fort for Joe.

Gotti did his walk and talk with Gravano. You could see them walking all over Little Italy so the feds couldn't use their surveillance equipment to pick up what they were talking about. Gotti, always eager to talk, wanted to find a place that was safe from the fed's bugs and listening devices. So John decided the home of the woman who lived upstairs from the hottest spot in the whole city, the Ravenite Social Club, was the safest place to talk.

Now John, Gravano, and Frankie Loc were making regular trips upstairs to talk. There was no doubt in my mind that Gravano and Frankie did not want to be upstairs at the Ravenite Club talking about things that had already happened.

But John liked to talk. "You know why I had Louie DiBono killed? He didn't come in when I sent for him." Or, "You know why I had this guy killed? You know why I had that guy killed?" He would go on and on.

First, a real boss that understands the Cosa Nostra doesn't talk about anyone they had killed. Why? Because what you're doing is bringing the guy you had killed back to life. The guy is dead, leave him dead. *Finito!* Talking about it only hurts you. It hurt John.

One of John's biggest faults was that he loved to talk and have the floor. And no one could have said anything because John was the boss. But what John didn't realize was that by going upstairs and talking he was killing all of them.

The feds had the Ravenite Club bugged for sound. Even the parking meters where John, Gravano, and Frankie walked and talked were bugged. The feds couldn't get enough from those bugged places to provide adequate evidence to arrest John. But as luck would have it, the feds got a tip that John went upstairs at the Ravenite Club to talk.

The woman who lived upstairs went to her daughter's home for the Thanksgiving holidays in November 1990. The feds took that opportunity to plant a couple of bugs in the apartment. Once the bugs were in place, the feds sat outside the Ravenite in a truck. They couldn't believe what they heard: Gambino boss, John Gotti, talking about murders.

On December 11, 1990, John, Gravano, and Frankie Loc—the whole administration—was indicted and arrested. At first, John laughed. He thought it was like all the other cases he'd had. But when they didn't make bail, he started to worry. When he found out the place upstairs was bugged, it was like the ceiling fell on his head.

As tough as John Gotti was, no one wants to spend the rest of his life in prison. But that's what the three Gambino men faced. John didn't need anyone to testify against him. Those tapes with his voice were sufficient evidence. Sometimes you can beat a federal government witness, but when it's your own voice talking on tape, it is hard to beat. You have only one option: get the tapes thrown out.

But the feds did everything just right. All the warrants were signed by a judge, so all the tapes were good. John, Gravano, and Frankie were held without bail. It didn't take Gravano long to start to cooperate. He was never any good anyway. All the money Gravano brought John had blinded John, or maybe John just didn't care about all the contract killings Gravano brought him.

The feds didn't need Gravano to testify against John. Those tapes were enough. What the feds wanted from Gravano was all the shooters hired on all the contract killings Gravano had done and where the

Gambino Family money came from. A lot of the money that came in went through Gravano's hands. Again, Gravano would like people to believe he turned bad because John betrayed him.

John used attorney Jerry Shargel. The only reason the feds got their way was because of another John Gotti mistake: making his attorneys Bruce Cutler and Jerry Shargel meet him at the Ravenite, which allowed the feds to succeed in declaring the two lawyers as house lawyers for the Gambino Family. I still believe the judge should have let Cutler and Shargel defend John. After all, John was fighting for his life, though nothing could have helped him. Those tapes were devastating. So John hired a lawyer out of Boston.

John and Frankie Loc went to trial, were convicted on all counts, and got life sentences with no parole. After all the men he had killed and all the families he had destroyed, Gravano got five years' time served. Where did Gravano do those five years? It took Gravano at least five years to testify against everyone. Maybe he was at an army base or a hotel, but believe me he never saw the inside of a prison. The feds treated Gravano like a star.

John would exhaust his appeals in 1994 and remained in prison until his death on June 10, 2002, at age sixty-one. Ironically, for a guy who liked to talk, John was diagnosed with throat and head cancer in 1998. His son

John Jr., reportedly said of his father's death, "If you look on his death certificate he choked on his own vomit and blood. He paid for his sins, and I think, at this point, I paid for it." John had dishonored the secret organization he swore his life to. The other Mafia families did not, as is customary, send a representative to his funeral. As for Frankie Loc, he's seventy-nine and remains in prison at a federal medical facility.

Chapter Fourteen

SINS OF THE FATHER

...I, THE LORD YOUR GOD, AM A JEALOUS GOD, PUNISHING THE CHILDREN FOR THE SIN OF THE FATHERS TO THE THIRD AND FOURTH GENERATION OF THOSE WHO HATE ME...–EXODUS 20:5

Back in 1988, John Gotti did something he said he would never do. He made his son John Gotti Jr. a wiseguy in the Gambino Family. After a short apprenticeship, John Jr. became a captain with his own crew. Some of his men were made, some were not. John Jr. loved every minute of it. Nobody forced him to do it or put a gun to his head.

When his father, Gravano, and Frankie Loc went to prison, John Jr. became the acting boss with the help of his uncle Pete Gotti. It was at that time that John Jr. got close with one of his father's soldiers, Bartholomew "Bobby" Boriello, the guy who had the

Chock full o' Nuts coffee shop. Bobby was made and put under John Jr. Then the two were together all the time.

A lot of the old-timers in the Gambino Family didn't like the idea of John Jr. being the acting boss with so little experience. What could he know about dealing with the bosses of other families? The bosses would turn him inside out. The old-timers were right. John Jr. didn't know how to be a boss.

The first mistake John Jr. made was making Michael "Mikey Scars" DiLeonardo, a captain. Again, Mikey was from Paul Castellano's side of the family and controlled all the construction from the family. So John Jr. made Mikey Scars a captain.

There was a disco in Brooklyn where John Jr. would go on a Friday night and hang out with Mikey Scars and his brother-in-law, Frankie Fappiano, a made member of the Gambino Family. Then John Jr. started going to a lot of dinners with Mikey Scars.

The mistake John Jr. made with Mikey Scars was the same mistake his father had made with Gravano. John Gotti had an army of good men out there in Queens and in Manhattan. He should have picked one of them to be underboss or captain. But that construction money had blinded him.

One night, Bobby Boriello returned home to Brooklyn and pulled into his driveway. His wife heard him get out of the car and say, "What are you doing here?" But Bobby didn't go into the house. When she went out to see where he was, she found him on the driveway, shot in the head.

Again, everyone thought it was a Gambino hit. Who would kill a Gambino soldier other than the Gambinos? When John Jr. found out about Bobby, he wanted to know who'd done it. First he got word to his father, who was still locked up in Brooklyn.

Word came back to John Jr. that Bobby was having trouble with an old friend who was a Genovese associate, Preston Geritano. He came up with Bobby in the old Gallo crew. Preston was a loner. He was a small guy but very dangerous with a gun. He liked to gamble but didn't like to pay. One day he went crazy. He went into a funeral parlor on Court Street in Brooklyn, took money off the owner, and told him he was under his protection and owed him protection money. He went into a car service on Smith Street, took the money out of the drawer and broke the place up. Both places were under Bobby Boriello's protection. Bobby, of course, tried to find Preston, but couldn't.

Bobby put all this on record with John Gotti Sr. So when Bobby got killed the first place John Jr. and Pete Gotti went to was the bosses of the Genovese Family. After a couple of meetings, the Genovese people proved Preston had been nowhere near Bobby's house when he was killed. When that happened, Preston had been working a numbers route. So he had to be at places at a set time every night. So the Genovese people checked with the people who Preston had to pick up. They found out that at the time Bobby was shot, Preston was on the other side of Brooklyn. He couldn't have been the man who shot Bobby.

So that meant three made men of the Gambino Family had been killed but not by them: Bobby Boriello, Eddie Lino, and Frankie DeCicco. John Gotti Sr. couldn't figure it out. Who would take a chance like that? If John had found out, it would have caused a war.

After Bobby's death, it was back to business. The money came rolling in. John Jr. was seen all the time with Mikey Scars. Word around the Gambino Family was that Mikey Scars was another Tommy Bolitti. Mikey Scars told John Jr. everything. If a soldier wasn't doing the right thing or if a soldier was doing the wrong thing, Mikey Scars would report it to John Jr. As you can imagine, Mikey Scars was not liked by all of the other members of the Gambino Family.

In the middle of 1998, John Jr. and a couple of his men were indicted. It was the usual RICO racketeering indictment, almost impossible to beat. John Jr. took a plea deal, which his father didn't like, but it was the smart thing. He took seventy-seven months at the Ray Brook Federal Correctional Institute in Upstate New York.

While John Jr. was away, Pete Gotti took over for the Gambino Family for his brother, John. Mikey Scars was still a captain, handling all the family's construction, and now he answered to Pete Gotti. Pete Gotti did a good job of running the family. In almost ten years at the top of the Gambino Family, Pete had no casualties under his leadership.

Just as John Jr. was finishing up his prison time, Mikey Scars and three other Gambino soldiers got indicted for the Weiss murder. Mikey Scars cooperated with the feds. Who did Mikey Scars give the most trouble? His friend and one-time boss, John Jr. So instead of getting ready to go home, John Jr. was brought to the Metropolitan Detention Center in Brooklyn and indicted on a murder conspiracy charge. The star witness against him was Mikey Scars. There were other witnesses against John Jr., but without Mikey Scars the feds would not have had a case.

By that time, John Gotti Sr. was in the US penitentiary in Marion, Illinois, doing life with no chance of parole. Meantime, Mikey Scars fingered his own brother-in-law, Frankie Fappiano, in two murders and his friend, Joey D'Angelo, in one murder. Both of those guys turned and testified against John Jr. But John Jr. got two hung juries. The judge let him out on bail. The feds and rats were upset that John Jr. was released.

The feds found some new guys to help testify, and John Jr. was indicted for a third time with Mikey Scars providing testimony. John Jr. got a third hung jury, but this time the judge threw the case out. So unless the feds came up with some new charges John Jr. was free. But it cost him and his family a lot of money and stress.

John Jr. should have left Mikey Scars alone, put him under one of his men instead of putting him in the construction money, or left him as a soldier. John Jr. made the same mistake his father made with Gravano. When Frankie DeCicco got killed, John should have built a wall between himself and anyone on Paul Castellano's side of the Gambino Family. He should have put in the administration one of his trusted men that stood next to him when he made the move on Paul. Gravano was a big earner for John. He handled a lot of the family's rackets, but when John made him underboss, he almost gave the Gambino Family back to Paul's side of the family. It should have been Frankie Loc instead of Gravano as underboss.

But it was always all about the money, not who was the best man for the job. John was a tough guy, a man who stood by what he believed. So, he stood in a cell locked up twenty-three hours a day for ten years. Then he died of cancer.

John took over the second largest mob family in New York, but he didn't know what to do with it. He hurt a lot of good men, and in the end he hurt himself. He had a five-year run as boss of the Gambino Family. In those five years, he had three federal cases, two of which he fixed and beat. But the last one he couldn't fix and it killed him.

But Gravano, the rat, got another chance in life. The feds let him take most of his millions of dollars to Arizona. He opened a construction business and did well, but that wasn't good enough for him. He went into the drug business with his son, Gerard, selling pills, ecstasy pills—millions of them. At that time, John Gotti was battling cancer and stepped down as boss. Pete Gotti became the official boss of the Gambino Family. It was much harder to take down an official boss and much easier to take down an acting boss.

In Arizona, Gravano was soon in trouble with the law again. He and his son got indicted for selling pills. Around that time, two Gambinos showed up in Arizona: one a soldier, Thomas "Huck" Carbonaro and the other an associate. Of course someone talked, and Pete Gotti and Huck were indicted for a murder conspiracy to kill Gravano.

Pete Gotti and Huck went to trial. The feds had a rat to testify that Pete Gotti ordered a hit on Gravano and that Huck and an associate were sent to

Arizona to kill Gravano. Pete Gotti and Huck were convicted. Huck had a life sentence and Pete got thirty-five years, which for him at seventy-three was the same as a life sentence.

Gravano went to trial for selling millions of pills. He was convicted and got twenty years while his son, Gerard, got ten years. Gravano had blown his second chance. With all the ratting and testifying he'd done about his life of crime, he had to go to prison anyway. If he'd wanted to die in prison like a man, he should have kept his mouth shut from the beginning, like his boss, John Gotti. But Gravano loved the money, and in the end it killed him.

Chapter Fifteen

WHO KILLED GOTTI'S GUYS?

Who killed Gotti's guys, Frankie DeCicco, Eddie Lino, and Bobby Boriello? It wasn't Gotti or anyone in the Gambino Family. But before we get to that, let's look at the Lucchese Family, one of the smaller of the Five Families in New York.

The Luccheses were always involved in drug dealing. They had an interest in both airports, JFK (John F. Kennedy International) and LaGuardia, and controlled the private sanitation on Long Island. In the 1970s, one of their captains was Christopher "Christie Tick" Furnari. He stayed on 14th Avenue and 86th Street in Brooklyn. He had a bar on the corner called the 19th Hole.

Christie's nights were Monday and Wednesday. He would arrive at the 19th Hole at 7:00 p.m. on those nights. Wiseguys and captains from all the families would come to see him. Some came to do business and some just to have a drink with Christie. He was well respected and a powerhouse in the Lucchese Family.

When the books opened in 1976, Christie put in two men to be made members of the Lucchese Family: Vittorio "Vic" Amuso and Anthony "Gaspipe" Casso. Both became made members under Christie in his crew. Both were close to him. Vic and Gaspipe were big earners. In the early '80s, the Lucchese boss, Anthony "Tony Ducks" Corallo, made Christie the family's consigliere. In turn, Christie made Vic a captain of his crew.

One of the guys around Christie was Fat Pete Chiodo. Christie called him his godson, but he never put Fat Pete up to be a made member of the family. He must have had his reasons. Not everyone is meant for the mob, especially these days.

When the bosses were convicted and sentenced to a hundred years each in the Commission case, the Lucchese bosses, Tony Ducks, Salvatore "Tom Mix" Santoro, and Christie stepped down and turned the leadership of the Lucchese Family over to Vic and Gaspipe. Vic became boss and Gaspipe underboss. Vic kept a low profile, but Gaspipe was always exposed and out front, dealing drugs, taking drugs, and killing people. Nobody was safe with Gaspipe around. His side kick was Fat Pete, so Gaspipe did something Christie wouldn't do: he made Fat Pete a member of the Lucchese Family in 1987.

It didn't take long before Fat Pete became a captain. It didn't make sense to a lot of people. Nobody would dare say anything about Gaspipe's choice, but I assure you Gaspipe wasn't thinking right when he made that choice. It turned out to be a big mistake for all of them. Most of the contracts to kill people went to Fat Pete and his crew.

Fat Pete was among the members of the other families who got arrested when the Windows case indictments came down. Fat Pete got bail as did most of the bosses. Vic and Gaspipe went on the lam, but they left Fat Pete and another captain, Alphonse "Little Al" D'Arco, in charge of the day-to-day running of the Lucchese Family.

At the time, Fat Pete was using drugs. He lost 100 pounds, put it back on, and then lost it again. He was also a liar. His word was no good. Other family members hated to meet with him. When Fat Pete and Little Al met with other family leaders, Fat Pete would get caught in his lies.

Little Al had his hands full with Fat Pete. Little Al couldn't complain about Fat Pete because Gaspipe loved him. Then word got back to Vic and Gaspipe that Fat Pete took a plea deal on the Windows indictment without telling anyone. Of course, that didn't sit well with them or the bosses of other families.

So Gaspipe gave Little Al the order to kill Fat Pete. Little Al sent his son, Joseph "Little Joe" D'Arco, and another wiseguy to kill Fat Pete. They found him at a gas station in Staten Island and they start shooting. Fat Pete had a gun on him. So both sides were shooting. Fat Pete got hit twelve times and lived. From the hospital bed he started to cooperate with the feds.

That was not good for anyone. Not only did Vic and Gaspipe have the Windows indictment over their heads, but now they had all kinds of murders. In the meantime, Little Al got scared for himself and his son because they'd fucked up the hit on Fat Pete and now Fat Pete was cooperating with the feds because of it.

Little Al knew how Gaspipe thought. Gaspipe would look to kill Little Al and his son. So Little Al and Little Joe cooperated with the feds. Now plenty of Lucchese wiseguys were going to be in trouble because Little Al was sharp as a whip.

The federal indictment ball started rolling toward the Luccheses because Fat Pete took a plea deal. Fat Pete should have never been a made member of the Lucchese Family. Gaspipe should have left him alone.

With new charges against them, Vic and Gaspipe could never come back. Both would have no chance at trial with Fat Pete and Little Al against them. Then the feds got a tip about a payphone that Vic used. Vic was arrested and held without bail. Gaspipe was caught in a house out in a woodsy rural area. He had guns and a couple hundred thousand dollars. Gaspipe was sent to the Metropolitan Correction Center in Manhattan and held without bail, but it wasn't long before he had a bunch of prison guards on his payroll. He was getting bags of food and drinks in his cell.

Gaspipe plotted an escape. His plan involved the van the jail guards used to transport prisoners to court appearances. Gaspipe's men were going to crash into the van. A guard he paid was supposed to give him keys to the van. But one of the guards Gaspipe was paying broke down and informed on the guards Gaspipe had on his payroll. They were arrested and Gaspipe's escape was foiled.

Gaspipe was put in the hole on twenty-three-hour lock-down. Sitting in the hole, knowing he was finished, Gaspipe decided to cooperate with the feds. Meanwhile, Vic went to trial, got convicted on all the murders, and received a couple of life sentences.

Gaspipe started to talk. When you cooperate with the feds, first you have to plead guilty to your whole indictment. Second, you have to admit to all of your crimes. If you don't tell the feds all of them and the crimes you didn't tell them later come out, your deal with the feds is done.

Three of the many murders Gaspipe admitted to committing were of Gotti's guys. First was DeCicco, the Gambino Family underboss. Gaspipe had a guy around him who made bombs, so it was he and this guy who put the bomb under DeCicco's car in hopes of killing Frankie and John. No official boss out there liked what Gotti and DeCicco did in assassinating Paul Castellano.

Second was the killing of Lino. Gaspipe said he used the two cops he had on his payroll. They pulled Lino over on the Belt Parkway and shot him dead. The third was Bobby Boriello. It was said that he was killed because of a drug deal with the Luccheses that went bad.

All this information went into a FD-302 form. Many of the gunmen that Gaspipe sent out on all his hits went to prison. Thanks to Fat Pete and Little Al cooperating, Gaspipe never took the stand against anyone. Why? Apparently the crimes Gaspipe admitted to were in direct contradiction with the testimony Gravano gave on his 302 and on the stand. So if Gaspipe took the stand it would be a matter of record, and then a defense lawyer could have used that contradictory evidence to get their client a new trial. So, the feds put Gaspipe in prison for the rest of his life. Again, what was John Gotti thinking when his underboss, Frankie DeCicco, was killed? When Eddie Lino, a captain, and Bobby Boriello, a soldier, were killed? John was the boss of the Gambino Family, but he never did anything about his men getting killed. The fact is, bosses are supposed to do something about it. John never did. He couldn't.

ᙅᙢᓂChapter Sixteenᙣᓂᙢ

BANANA SPLITS

Joe Bonanno, the boss of what we called the Banana Family, was a young, sharp boss. But Bonanno made a mistake forming an alliance with the new boss of the Profaci Family, Joe Profaci's brother-in-law, Joe Magliocco. He took over when Profaci died of cancer on June 6, 1962.

Bonanno and Magliocco decided to kill bosses Carlo Gambino and Tommy Lucchese. Magliocco sent one of his captains, Joe Colombo, to kill Gambino, but instead Colombo told Gambino about the plot to kill him and Lucchese.

When word got out about Colombo's duplicity, Magliocco died of a heart attack and Bonanno fled to Arizona. The bosses gave the Profaci Family to Colombo, who renamed it after himself, and the Bonanno Family fell into disarray.

The failed power play by Bonanno and Magliocco caused a split in the family between Bonanno loyalists and those who opposed what Colombo had done. A lot of shooting and killing went on until the middle of the 1970s when Phillip "Rusty" Rastelli took over and put the Bonanno Family back together.

A few years later, Rusty was convicted for racketeering and got twenty years in federal prison. One of his soldiers was in with him, Joe Massino. When Massino came home, he stayed loyal to Rusty, but the Bonanno Family split again: some were loyal to Rusty, the boss, and others were loyal to Carmine "Lilo" Galante.

It was during this time, late '70s early '80s, with the family at its weakest, that Joe Pistone aka Donnie Brasco, an FBI agent, infiltrated the Bonannos. Pistone got close to the weakest crew and its captain, Dominick "Sonny Black" Napolitano. Just before Pistone joined with Benjamin "Lefty Guns" Ruggiero, a Bonanno soldier under Sonny Black, Lilo was killed. He had gone around like he was the boss, and then he was dead.

That left Massino and his men, loyalists to Rusty and Alphonse "Sonny Red" Indelicato, the underboss who opposed Rusty. A meeting was setup to make peace and put the Bonanno Family back together, again.

Sonny Red and one of his captains, Philip "Philly Lucky" Giaccone, were to meet Massino and a couple of his captains in a social club in Bensonhurst on May 5, 1981. Another captain, Dominick "Big Trin" Trinchera, drove Sonny Red and Philly Lucky to the meeting. When they arrived, Massino, his brother-in-law, Sally Vitale, who was a captain at the time, and another captain, Frankie Lino, were there waiting.

Instead of making peace, Massino opened fire as soon as Sonny Red, Philly Lucky, and Big Trin were in the club. All three were killed, hauled into in a van driven by James "Big Louie" Tartaglione, and then taken somewhere and buried.

When word of the murders got out, the fed's pulled Pistone off the street. If Pistone had known any of that was going on, all of those guys would have been arrested immediately. That Sonny Black and his crew were in the dark meant Pistone was too.

Because of Pistone's infiltration of the Bonanno Family, a lot of wiseguys went to prison. Also because of Pistone, Tony Mirra and Sonny Black were killed. The only reason Lefty Guns wasn't killed was because he was one of the men Pistone put away. Lefty got twenty-five years in federal prison, where he died.

When Massino was again convicted for racketeering and sent to prison for ten years, he made Sally Vitale his underboss and kept Anthony Spero as his consigliere because Spero was a Rusty man. He made Big Louie Tartaglione a captain. Then Rusty passed away in prison and Massino became the official boss of the Bonanno Family.

After John Gotti killed Paul Castellano and took over the Gambino Family in late 1985, Massino sent word from jail, where he was awaiting trial for racketeering, to Sally Vitale to stay close to Gotti. After the FBI infiltration, the Bonanno Family was thrown off the Commission. John, as one of the most powerful bosses in New York, tried to get Massino and the Bonannos reinstated, but the Commission refused. Eventually, after the other four families' leadership had been decimated because of the Commission trial, Massino took a seat on the board.

Massino was just finishing his three years supervised release when Gotti went to prison in April of 1992. It was time for Massino to rebuild the Bonanno Family and put them back on the map of organized crime. He hired men that he thought were men of honor and trust. He made Frank Coppa a captain. He made Richie "Shellackhead" Cantarella a captain and a liaison between the other families and the Bonanno Family. He made Vinny Basciano a captain. Basciano in turn made his best friend, Dominick Cicale, a made member of the Bonanno Family.

Then the fun started. Massino was in for some surprises once the feds started arresting members of the Bonanno Family.

Sally Vitale, now an underboss, got arrested for bank fraud. Big Louie Tartaglione got indicted for racketeering. Massino made Richie Cantarella acting underboss until Sally Vitale got out of prison. Sally Vitale was looking at thirty-three months, but the feds were putting a case together with the murders of Sonny Red, Philly Lucky, and Big Trin. In 2003, Sally Vitale rolled over and cooperated with the feds.

Next, Massino, Lino, Coppa, and Joe D'Amico, a soldier in the Bonanno Family, are indicted, thanks to Sally Vitale. Their charges were murder. When Sonny Red, Philly Lucky, and Big Trin were killed, Sally Vitale was right there next to Massino.

Lino was charged with killing Sonny Black. He brought Sonny Black to a meeting where Lino pushed Sonny Black down the stairs. At the bottom was a Bonanno soldier, Bobby Lino Sr., Frankie's cousin, who shot Sonny Black in the head. D'Amico was charged with killing his cousin, Tony Mirra. Massino was charged with all of those murders.

In the meantime, Basciano took over the Bonanno Family as acting boss for Massino, who was held in MDC without bail. Basciano made Cicale a captain. Massino's codefendants—Lino, D'Amico, and Coppa—became witnesses for the government. Massino sat at the defense table by himself.

Next, Cantarella, his son, and his wife got arrested. Cantarella turned for the feds. Then Bonanno consigliere Spero got convicted for murder and racketeering. He died in prison doing his time. Big Louie Tartaglione was finishing up his sentence when the feds told him, "We know you drove the van that took the bodies of Sonny Red, Philly Lucky, and Big Tri." He decided to cooperate and wore a wire for more than two years.

In July 2004, Massino's trial ended and he got convicted. All of his guys took the stand against him. Basciano was running the Bonanno Family, and who was he meeting with all that time? Big Louie and his wire. Massino got life with no chance for parole. The feds kept out one murder, Randy Pizzolo, who was killed in 2004, because they could charge Massino with ordering a contract killing, which would have allowed the government to seek the death penalty if Massino was convicted.

The government had confiscated $11 million of Massino's assets, his house where his wife and children lived, his mother's house, and a couple of businesses they owned. Once Massino was sentenced, he was held at MDC Brooklyn in solitary for twenty-three hours a day. When the feds take Big Louie off the street, they locked up Basciano and thirty other wiseguys and captains.

Why didn't anybody realize what Big Louie was doing? He was on three years' supervised release. He wasn't legally allowed to hang around wiseguys. He could go right back to prison for it. Big Louie put a dent in the Bonannos.

In 2007, Basciano and Cicale, his best friend, were on trial for murder. In the middle of the trial, Cicale turned and testified against Basciano. Basciano lost two trials. For one he got twenty years, and for the second, in 2011, he got life without parole. At MDC he was put upstairs with Massino. When Big Louie taped Basciano, Basciano was recorded saying, "I'm only helping our friend, Joe Massino." Then he said, "I know I am going from the frying pan into the fire. I have no axes to grind, he is our boss."

The Christmas before Basciano got arrested in 2005, he sent Massino's wife $50,000. He was the only one who looked out for his boss. Then Massino turned for the feds and started wearing a wire in 2005 to trap Basciano. Massino got one of the guards to move Basciano into the same cell with him. Massino, wearing a wire, said to Basciano, "You had to kill Randy Pizzolo? There was no other way?" Massino was showing that he did not give the order to kill

Pizzolo. It was Basciano. Basciano said Randy was out of control and wouldn't listen to anyone; he was disrespectful to other wiseguys, and it also sent a good message to everyone. Then he told Massino, "The prosecutor who prosecuted both of us is dead; we are going to kill him."

All of this was on tape. Massino must have jumped for joy. Basciano got charged with ordering the hit on Pizzolo and Massino's family got to keep a lot of the money and assets the government had confiscated.

Basciano faced the death penalty, if convicted. All the Bonanno guys made deals to help themselves and the government. So who paid for killing Sonny Red, Philly Lucky, Big Trin, Sonny Black, and Tony Mirra? Massino ordered all those guys killed. How could the government deal with him?

Basciano went on trial for killing Pizzolo in 2011. The star witness against him was Massino. When Massino was on the stand, he testified that the Commission had become a joke. He said the Five Families hadn't met since 1985, just before Paul Castellano was killed. Massino lamented that when he convened the meeting of the mob leaders in January of 2000, a motley crew showed up: Louis "Louie Bagels" Daidone, acting boss of the Lucchese's who is now doing life with no parole; Pete Gotti, Gambino boss, who is now doing twenty-five years; Joe Waverly, Colombo consigliere, who is now doing twenty-five years; and Little Larry Dentico, Genovese consigliere, who is ninety years old. These bosses are men. Massino is the motley one.

The jury returned a guilty verdict against Basciano on May 16, 2011. At the penalty phase, they had to decide whether to have Basciano executed or imprisoned for life with no chance for parole. On June 1, 2011, the jury gave him life instead of death by lethal injection. The jurors reasoned that other murderous mobsters did not get the death sentence.

Massino, now seventy, walked out of prison after serving more than ten years for seven murders because of his help convicting Basciano. He's now in the witness protection program, a free man.

‹♦›Chapter Seventeen‹♦›

THE FAMILY OF FAMILIES

C harlie "Lucky" Luciano was probably the smartest mobster to walk the streets of New York City. In 1931, he created the Five Families, which have lasted more than eighty years. He handpicked their bosses. His family was the strongest. They had the most members and the most money. Lucky Luciano was boss, Vito Genovese was underboss, and Frank Costello was consigliere.

Lucky had one of the toughest Jewish mobsters at his side, Benjamin "Bugsy" Siegel, and one of the smartest Jewish mobsters, Meyer Lansky, a big earner. Together, Lucky and Meyer made untold money. Lucky made one big mistake: he went into prostitution. Vito Genovese was against it. But Lucky went ahead, got arrested and went to trial. He lost his case and received fifty years in prison.

When World War II broke out, Lucky, from prison, helped the country keep order on the Manhattan docks. He thought that would free him. It did. He was deported to Italy and never again returned to the United States.

Lucky left Frank Costello as the acting boss of the Luciano Family with Vito as the underboss. Vito wasn't happy with that arrangement and plotted to take control. It took him ten years. He had Albert Anastasia, the boss of the Gambino Family, killed and sent his protégé, Vincent "Chin" Gigante, to kill Costello. Costello, of course, lived and stepped down. Vito took over what was then the Genovese Family. He was the most powerful and most feared boss in the country. He picked Michele "Big Mike" Miranda as his consigliere and a New Jersey man, Gerardo "Jerry" Catena, as his underboss.

Vito loved the West Village where he had one of his strongest crews. The captain who controlled it for him was Anthony "Tony Bender" Strollo. Chin Gigante was under Tony Bender. Another village captain was Thomas "Tommy Ryan" Eboli. He controlled the boxing in New York. You had to go through Tommy Ryan to get a title fight.

In Brooklyn, Vito had five crews. Out of the five crews, the most powerful of them was under Alphonse Frank "Funzi" Tiere. He stood on 64th Street and 20th Avenue at Tony's Cafe. Then there was Cosmo "Gus" Frasca on 14th Avenue and 66th Street. On Cropsey Avenue there was Little Danny. On Utrecht Avenue there was Mike Generoso Sr.

In Williamsburg, there was another feared captain, Pasquale "Patty Mac" Macciarole. Vito also had an army of men in Harlem. One of the most powerful captains was Philip "Benny Squint" Lombardo. Also, there was Fat Tony Salerno. Between the two of them they must have had one hundred or more soldiers. Philip Lombardo's right-hand man was Antonio "Buckaloo" Ferro. They had everything in Harlem locked up.

In 1958, when Vito was indicted for drug trafficking, things changed in the Genovese Family. Vito went to trial, got convicted, and received fifteen years. He was sent to the Atlanta Federal Penitentiary.

Vito made Tommy Ryan acting boss. A lot of the men didn't like Tommy Ryan. At the time, Mike Miranda was dying. Vito's brother was a soldier in the family, so messages were sent to Tommy Ryan from Vito's brother. Tommy Ryan didn't care for Tony Bender, the captain of the West Village. Tommy Ryan told Vito some bad stories about Tony Bender. Tony Bender disappeared. A lot of men under Tony Bender didn't like it. Time passed. On February 14, 1969, Vito Genovese died in prison.

Tommy Ryan thought it was his time to take over the Genovese Family, but Benny Squint Lombardo, Jerry Catena, and Chin Gigante had other ideas. Sometime in 1972, Tommy Ryan was coming out of his girlfriend's house when he was gunned down.

Lombardo, Catena, and Gigante got together. Benny Squint became the boss. Gigante became captain of the West Village. They handpicked three men to be the official administration of the Genovese Family: Funzi Tiere became the front boss and Fat Tony Salerno, the underboss. Benny Squint picked his right-hand man as consigliere, Buckaloo Ferro.

If any bosses from the other families wanted to see the Genovese people, they would meet with Funzi, Buckaloo, or Fat Tony. Benny Squint was well off as the real boss. He only wanted to know if someone had to get killed. He would give the ok to a contract, but only if it was a very good reason. That is why those men lasted so long as bosses. Money wasn't Benny Squint's or Gigante's god. What belonged to them as bosses belonged to them; they wanted their soldiers to make money.

When the books opened in 1976 and the Genovese Family put men in for membership, Buckaloo did most of the running around. He would go to Brooklyn if needed. Most of the other families had an induction ceremony and would have their boss, underboss, and consigliere there, but not the Genovese Family. Why jeopardize all the bosses at one time?

The Genovese believed that new soldiers needed to know only their captain. Funzi was a greedy boss, but only in Brooklyn where he stood. If Brooklyn captains brought him money, he would take it, where Benny Squint and Gigante would refuse it. Benny Squint would meet a handful of guys that he chose to see. It would be at one o'clock in the morning at the Stage Deli in Manhattan. The Stage Deli was open twenty-four hours a day, seven days a week.

When Benny Squint wanted to send a message to Gigante, he would send Sammy Salerno and Fat Tony would send Vincent "Fish" Cafaro. Sometimes you would see the two of them on Sullivan Street talking to Gigante.

Patty Mac, the captain from Williamsburg, didn't respect Funzi as the boss. He wouldn't show up to meetings that Funzi would call. He would go on vacation without checking in. One day in 1979, they found Patty Mac in a car trunk with his head blown off.

In the late '70s, after more than sixty years in the Mafia, Meyer Lansky was living in Miami, Florida. He was close with a Genovese captain, Vincent "Jimmy Blue Eyes" Alo. Once a year Benny Squint and Jerry Catena would go down to Miami and stay a couple of months. The four old-timers, Benny, Jerry, Meyer, and Jimmy Blue Eyes, would get together.

From time to time Funzi would be seen checking in with Benny Squint up in Harlem or down in the village with Gigante, so it was obvious that Funzi wasn't calling the shots. Back when all of this was going on, law enforcement didn't know anything about that. Funzi was just the front boss of the Genovese Family. Yet, his picture appeared on the cover of *Time* magazine, "Boss of all Bosses." Everyone was apparently fooled.

When the books opened in 1976, a lot of good men were inducted into the Genovese Family. Benny Squint and Buckaloo put in Sammy Salerno (no relation to Fat Tony). Fat Tony put in Fish Cafaro.

In the summer of 1978, Buckaloo suffered a massive heart attack and died. He was fifty-six years old. The wake was held in the Bronx. Anyone who was anyone showed up at Buckaloo's wake to show respect. After Buckaloo was buried, Benny Squint and Gigante made Gigante's partner, Dominick "Fat Dom" Alongi, consigliere of the Genovese Family.

Not long after his promotion, Fat Dom went to Florida and died of a heart attack. He was waked at a funeral parlor on Sullivan Street. The consigliere job opened again. This time Benny Squint and Gigante put one of Gigante's captains in the spot, Louis "Bobby" Manna. Then Funzi got indicted in 1980 and one of the charges against him was being the boss of the Genovese Family. He got convicted in January 1981 and was sentenced to ten years. He died of cancer in March of that year.

So the Genovese people upped Fat Tony to boss and one of Benny Squint's men, Sammy Salerno, to underboss. In 1980, Benny Squint's health started to fail. He started getting mini strokes and spent a lot of time in Florida. In April 1987, Benny Squint passed away. Then Chin Gigante became the boss.

When a big construction indictment came down, Fat Tony, Fish Cafaro, and Sammy Salerno were arrested. Fat Tony and Fish were held without bail. Sammy Salerno got out on bail and died of a heart attack. Some people said he killed himself. He was caught on tape talking in the social club about the bosses. In the late 1980s, Louis "Bobby" Manna, the consigliere, got indicted for plotting to kill John Gotti. He had opposed Gotti's killing of Paul Castellano. Bobby got eighty years, effectively life in prison without parole.

By then Gigante had no choice but to put one of his close men, Venero "Benny Eggs" Mangano, up front. At the time, Gotti was still running around as the Gambino boss and saying, "Where is the administration of the Genovese Family? What do they mean Benny Eggs is it?"

Meantime, Fat Tony had a falling out in jail with Fish. Fat Tony had all the numbers business in Harlem. He did a half a million dollars per week. Fish ran it for him. But when Fat Tony and Fish were locked up, a lot of the money Fish handled came up short. So one day in jail, Fat Tony confronted Fish and went after him with his cane. The guards had to place them on different floors. Fish soon started to cooperate with the feds. At the time, the feds had locked up all the bosses in the Commission case. Fat Tony was indicted as a Genovese boss. He was basically done.

For the first time the feds had the real story on the Genovese Family and it came from Fish. If the feds had doubts about Gigante being the boss, Fish set them straight. Gigante, because of Fish, started to get plenty of attention from the feds. In 1990, Gigante got indicted in the Windows case with some other bosses. He made bail because of his health. Benny Eggs was also arrested in the Windows case. So, Gigante picked Barney Bellomo from Harlem as acting boss, Jimmy Ida as consigliere, and an old-timer from Brooklyn, Michele "Mickey Domino" Generoso as underboss. They ran the family pretty well.

Barney would send his men out to little diners in Manhattan and have them take cards with the name and addresses of the diners. When he wanted to see somebody, one of his men would go to the man in the daytime and give him a card with a time of the appointment on the back. Most of the time, the appointment was after midnight. Sometimes a person would show up for the appointment and somebody would be waiting for him at a restaurant and take him to another place to meet Barney. Barney was very careful.

Unfortunately, Barney, Mickey, and Jimmy would meet with three men who eventually turned rat and cooperated with the feds: Sammy the Bull Gravano of the Gambino Family, Little Al D'Arco of the Lucchese Family, and Carmine Sessa of the Colombo Family.

On June 11, 1996, Barney, Mickey, and Jimmy were indicted on RICO charges. The front page of the next Sunday's *New York Post* read, "All The Chin's Men." Barney and Mickey took plea deals. Barney got ten years, and Mickey, because of his age, got twenty-four months. Jimmy went to trial, lost, and received a life sentence.

In 1997, the feds took Gigante to trial in the Windows case. He lost and was sentenced to twelve years in prison where he died in 2005 of natural causes. Chin Gigante was seventy-seven years old.

Of the Five Families, the Genovese have had the least number of members cooperate with the government—eight—and none of them in leadership. Genovese soldier Joe Valachi was the first to confirm the existence of the Mafia in 1963 and provided details of its history, operations, and rituals, though his testimony never led directly to the prosecution of any Mafia bosses. The Bonanno Family had fourteen informants, including a boss, Joe Massino, an underboss, and an acting underboss; the Gambino Family had twelve, including Gravano, the underboss;

the Lucchese Family had fifteen, including three acting bosses, Anthony "Gaspipe" Casso, Little Al D'Arco, and Joseph "Little Joe" Defede; and the Colombo Family had seventeen informants, including consigliere Carmine Sessa and nine capos or acting capos.

Chapter Eighteen

MAFIA TWILIGHT?

What made the Italian Mafia strong during its long reign? They controlled all the rackets in New York City and New Jersey. The unions, the docks, private sanitation, the Fulton Fish Market, and the garment district were all mob controlled. The Mafia was also well organized and disciplined, and they used the instrument of fear to maintain control.

If a captain who controlled one of those rackets died, the next wiseguy that took his place would inherit it. The Fulton Fish Market was controlled by the Genovese Family for fifty years. Bosses got their cut, but the racket always belonged to the family, not one individual.

Big money for the bosses came from the unions and the docks. In the early years, Albert Anastasia had the docks in Brooklyn. When he was killed, Carlo Gambino got them. When Carlo died, Paul Castellano got them. After John Gotti assassinated Paul in 1985, John got them. The government finally took them over with a lot of help from informants.

The feds will work with anyone willing to cooperate. It doesn't matter if you killed a hundred guys as long as you can give them mob guys. There's a problem with this, especially when you consider Bonnano boss, Joe Massino, who was convicted of killing seven guys, and then got to walk free after cooperating with the feds.

There should be a law that if you are arrested and want to cooperate, especially if you pulled the trigger, you still should have to do twenty years. The break you would get would be that you don't get life. Then see how many wiseguys would cooperate. Some of these guys don't want to do ten minutes in lockup.

It's a domino effect, and it's killing the Mafia. It goes like this: The captain in a mob family gives an order to two soldiers to go out and kill a guy. Down the road the captain gets indicted but doesn't want to go to prison, so he cooperates with the feds and gives up the two soldiers who he sent on the hit. Two guys are in prison because their captain put them there. Why should a wiseguy trust a captain anymore?

Worse for the Mafia is when the boss of a family rats out his own people. Massino cooperated with the government because he had been convicted of murder and faced the death penalty. So, he ratted out dozens of guys and went free. Massino's ratting almost sent another guy, Vincent Bascino, to his death. The jury gave Bascino life instead. Now, why should a wiseguy respect a boss anymore? And how's a boss going to instill fear or demand discipline when no one respects him? A criminal organization can't succeed this way. No organization can.

Until the end of the 1970s, you never saw the kind of betrayal that led made members of the Mafia to wear wires or bosses rolling over and testifying against their own men. Who could anyone trust? This is what will end organized crime, the distrust men have of each other, not the feds' arrests and convictions.

Back in the days when New York had neighborhoods that were mostly Italian, the old guys would bring young guys up in the life. The old guys would know the young guys' mothers, fathers, and grandparents for years. That's how I got into the Mafia. But those days are long gone.

In the Mafia today, here's what we're up against: The feds have their investigations of organized crime down to a science. They have an effective legal tool, the RICO statute. They have technology that makes it difficult to go anywhere and talk in private. They know more about the life and the mob business than most wiseguys. There is always someone—an associate, a soldier, a captain, a boss— looking to talk to the government, to inform against other wiseguys, to turn rat.

The Mafia was once a secret organization, but its secrets are known and its instrument of control, fear, is gone. Everyone knows about the Mafia. New York's Five Families are on television and the Internet, in countless books (including this one), magazines, newspapers, and movies.

Joining the mob is not like what it used to be. Back in the '70s and into the early '80s, a street guy that had businesses like the numbers game, sports betting, joker poker machines, or loan-sharking wanted to get inducted into the Mafia to become a made man so he could protect all his businesses from other made men.

When you start out as an associate with the Mafia you have to answer to a made man. He protects you and your businesses; most of the time you would have to cut him in on your businesses' earnings. When you are a made man you handle your own problems. You can protect the guys that are close to you. Many things have changed.

Back in the '70s, I would estimate, there were more than 3,000 wiseguys running around New York. Today, there are less than 500 of us. The smart ones are laid back, not looking to go to prison. Two of the Five Families are almost finished: the Colombo and Bonanno families. Fighting among factions in a family and between families is over. Now they're fighting not to go to jail.

The government took the mob-run businesses. Lotto replaced the numbers game. You can play a "Pick Three" game twice a day, once at twelve thirty in the afternoon and again at 7:30 p.m. It pays $500 on a dollar. Joker poker machines are done. You can't lend money to anyone on the vig anymore. After a while people stop paying you, and if you pressure them to pay, they run to the feds. It's the same with sports betting.

The feds have taken control of the docks in New York and corporations have moved into other big enterprises such as waste hauling and pornography. When made men took control of a family as John Gotti and Joe Colombo did, they inherited money-making empires. Today, there are no more empires.

People are no longer afraid of the Mafia. When they get in a jam with wiseguys they go to the feds. Back in the '70s people were afraid of the Mafia. If you had a problem there was always someone you could go to who would talk for you. No more. Other ethnic groups have no respect for wiseguys. The Albanians, the Russians, and the Chinese—they had respect for the Mafia back in the day. No more.

Money is the root of all evil, and, just like everywhere else, money has been a problem in the Mafia. Greed made guys make bad decisions; greed landed some guys in prison; greed got some guys killed.

Fifteen years from now, I don't think there will be anything to talk about.

The Mafia will be gone.

THE END

CPSIA information can be obtained at www.ICGtesting.com
Printed in the USA
BVOW08s2137280316

442078BV00001B/9/P